"It should be our purpose to grow inspired, concerned, loving people. An inspired, concerned and loving society will dignify man; will find the ways to develop his talent; will put the fruits of his labor and intellect to effective use; will achieve brotherhood; eliminate bigotry and intolerance, will care for the indigent, the delinquent, the sick, the aged, seek the truth and communicate it; respect differences among men."

James Rouse, 1963

COLUMBIA

A Celebration

Photographs by David Hobby

Text by Susan Thornton Hobby

perry Publishing

The Columbia Association maintains more than one-hundred forty tot lots and play areas scattered throughout the villages.

Published by: Perry Publishing
               5087 Columbia Road
               Columbia, MD 21044
               410-997-2731

Library of Congress Catalog Card Number 95-70208

ISBN 0-9643728-1-9

Printed in Canada through: PSA Graphics
                            5161 Columbia Road
                            Columbia, Maryland 21044
                            410-964-9809

ACKNOWLEDGMENTS

Inevitably, many more people contribute to the making of a book than those that can be listed on its spine. We would like to thank James Rouse, for envisioning the city in which we live and for devoting his time to our project; Ginny Edwards and Barbara Kellner of the Columbia Archives for their research and patience; Rich Riggins and Chris Usher for their photographic judgment; Carrie Brown for her guidance, editing and encouragement; Amy Bolton for her perfectionism; Marsha and Perry Berman for their enthusiasm, faith and hard work; and our families and employer, Patuxent Publishing Co., for their tolerance and support. A generous dose of gratitude is also due to all those people who told us their stories and invited us into their homes and businesses.

THE CONTENTS

INTRODUCTION

*C*olumbia began as an espionage operation.

In February of 1963, large tracts of Howard County farm land suddenly began disappearing into the hands of unknown buyers. Beneath layers of subterfuge and anonymity, behind false corporations and mysterious contracts, someone was quickly amassing an astonishing number of acres. Someone was buying land. And lots of it.

Rumors spread. The U.S. government was acquiring land to build a laboratory to test tropical diseases, or to turn Howard County into a giant landfill. The money came from the Soviet Union, farmers whispered.

But there was no dastardly plan. The benign mastermind behind the land acquisition was James Rouse, a small-town boy turned real estate developer. And he wanted to build a city.

Not just an ordinary city, either, but a planned community, one which would take into account — and seek to avoid — the errors of runaway suburban development and growing urban blight. Rouse wanted to build a better city. And with $23 million promised from interested backers, he started hiring lawyers to buy the land he needed.

Tacked to a wall of The Rouse Company headquarters in the Village of Cross Keys in Baltimore was a map of thirty-thousand acres of Howard County, the geographic bridge of farm land between Baltimore and Washington, D.C., two old and established cities creeping toward each other as they grew. Those fields of corn and horse pasture were the perfect site for Rouse's dreams.

"When we were buying this land, they had no idea who was buying it," says Rouse today, more than a quarter-century after that first settlement, sitting at the end of an old farm table in his office overlooking downtown Columbia. "But higher and higher prices were being paid. We bought all the land that was for sale for $500 an acre, and then $700, then we went to $1,000.

"We had counted on it taking three years, but we found as we bought land... automatically there was word out that there were a lot of people buying land in Howard County. Of course," Rouse says, chuckling, "we were all the people."

(Left) James Rouse

THE DISCOVERY

PUSHPIN

GEIST'S
PLAINS

VEN'S FOREST RESURVEYED

LITTLE

HO

THE DISCOVERY

OWEN BROWN RD.

RICHMOND'S
LOTT

HUNTING GROUND

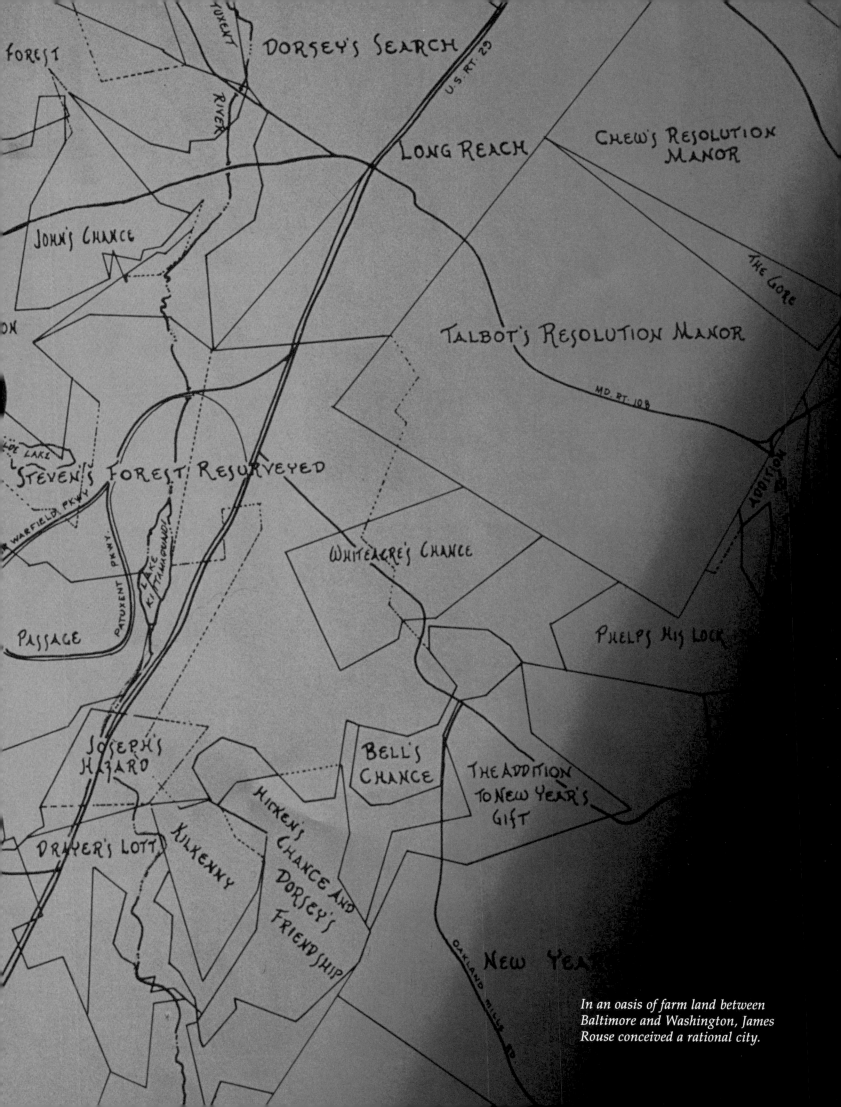

FOREST

DORSEY'S SEARCH

TUXENT

RIVER

U.S. RT 29

LONG REACH

CHEW'S RESOLUTION MANOR

JOHN'S CHANCE

THE GORE

TALBOT'S RESOLUTION MANOR

MD. RT. 108

LAKE

STEVEN'S FOREST RESURVEYED

WARFIELD PKWY

PATUXENT PKWY

LAKE KITTAMAQUNDI

WHITEACRE'S CHANCE

PHELPS HIS LOCK

PASSAGE

JOSEPH'S HAZARD

BELL'S CHANCE

THE ADDITION TO NEW YEAR'S GIFT

HICKEN'S CHANCE AND DORSEY'S FRIENDSHIP

DRAPER'S LOTT

KILKENNY

OAKLAND MILLS RD.

NEW YEAR

In an oasis of farm land between Baltimore and Washington, James Rouse conceived a rational city.

Lawyers often offered farmers life estates —
allowing them to live and work their property
until their deaths. One contract even stated that
the owners had the farm as long as they and
their horse lived, Rouse recalls. If the property
owners chose to take their money and run, The
Rouse Company hired tenant farmers to plant
and harvest crops until the plan was approved
and land grading started. "We became the big-
gest farmers in the state of Maryland," Rouse
says. "We couldn't just let the farms sit there."

But some people refused to sell, creating isolated chunks of farm land surrounded
by the growing maze of Rouse's planned development. Some hold-out parcels still exist
within the finished framework of what has become Columbia. The Rouse Company couldn't
persuade the owner of a large stone house to
sell the property on the shores of what became
Wilde Lake, for instance, though property owners on either side of the old home agreed to turn
over title to Rouse. As workers surveyed and
dug sewer lines, the owner of the house would
"stand on her porch with a rifle in her hand,
and defy anybody to step on her property. We
had to go around that property with the greatest care," Rouse recalls.

By April, 1963, Rouse finally had in hand
$23 million from Connecticut General, the com-
pany headed by Frazar Wilde, a Hartford insurance executive who believed in Rouse — his
vision, and his promised profits.

In the fourteen-thousand acres that was to become Columbia, some Howard County land owners refused to sell, leaving a few scattered farms within the surrounding city.

The Promised Land

The same summer that Martin Luther King Jr. envisioned all God's children living together in freedom, James Rouse began realizing his own dream. Based partly on the garden cities of England and the new town movement in California, Rouse's city would house one-hundred and ten thousand people in an area the size of the island of Manhattan. Free from sprawl and the social evils Rouse hoped to vanquish by giving people a better place to live, his city would grow better people, Rouse believed.

In October, 1963, The Rouse Company took its idea of a "rational city" to Howard County's three Republican commissioners, men who had been elected on an anti-growth platform. By then, The Rouse Company had bought fourteen-thousand acres in what was to be Columbia, vast conglomerated parcels surrounding thirteen existing subdivisions with six-thousand five-hundred residents.

For the next eighteen months, in a grueling round of presentations, Rouse executives attended meetings to put their plans before PTAs, farm bureaus, church congregations and political groups. Sometimes, the questioning by residents became hostile, Rouse remembers.

"I made a rule then that anybody being asked a question should assume that the person asking it was a good friend who was misadvised," Rouse says. "And therefore this would always be our manner of dealing with any question. We would never regard them as an enemy. We really stuck to that. We just never were provoked. I think that mattered a great deal. The potential fires were put out before they were ever lit."

Rouse had learned this approach developing the Village of Cross Keys in Roland Park, a proud old community in north Baltimore. The company devised a plan, and then convinced the neighbors that it would improve their lives and enhance their property values. It worked. And it worked in Columbia, too.

As The Rouse Company began dampening the fires of resistance in rural Howard County, company executives, with Jim Rouse at their helm, were busy planning the nuts and bolts of their new city.

Rouse summoned to Baltimore a group of fourteen educators, social scientists and experts on urban life to brainstorm about the new town. At first, the consultants

Columbia's People Tree, and the walk surrounding it made from bricks that Columbia's families and businesses sponsored, are the centerpiece for the Kittamaqundi Lakefront. Pierre duFayet's sculpture has become a symbol of the town's philosophy.

were pessimistic. The obstacles to creating what Rouse called a "humane" city were almost insurmountable — expense, social prejudice, government regulation.

Then, Chester Rapkin, a University of Pennsylvania professor of city planning, turned the experts around. He and Rouse started talking about this new city in terms no one except the utopian planners of the nineteenth century had ever used before.

The city, Rapkin said, should be conceived in love. And with that abstract foundation, the group moved forward to design a city that would reflect a social conscience determined to address not just the practical needs of its residents, but also its spiritual ones — villages cozily encircling community centers and elementary schools, counseling centers on bus routes, meditation benches along the bike paths.

And Rouse decided to call his city "Columbia"— because it had an "hallelujah sound to it."

Slowly, the plans began to emerge on paper and blueprints — cul-de-sacs and village centers and man-made lakes. The first plans were posted in Smith House, an old mansion on Route 29. Almost ten-thousand people came to see them. Gradually, the farmers and suburbanites were won over. When Rouse presented the county commissioners with the final eight-by-eight-foot model in November, 1964, he told them, "We want to stimulate not fear but hope. We see this not as a threat but as an opportunity."

He remembers the reaction from the audience. "Here was this county that had never had a rowhouse, that never had a garden apartment, that was opposed to development, all development," Rouse says. "When they called upon the opposition, after we'd made our presentation, nobody, not one person in Howard County, opposed the zoning. Astonishing, for forty-five thousand people. So it works, if you respect people and if you also genuinely believe that what you're doing is right, not wrong, not abusive, not greedy. People are apt to be for it."

Though the county commissioners were not completely sold, the community at large eventually came to The Rouse Company's rescue. When the commissioners tried to block the plan on a legal technicality, Howard County organizations like the League of Women Voters and the farm bureau lobbied for the new city. The commissioners capitulated when they saw their constituents standing behind the idea of Columbia. The necessary zoning permits were granted in

"Columbia gave me an opportunity to see people as they could really be at their greatest moments," remembers Maggie Brown, now a vice president of the Columbia Association.

August, 1965.

"I think the only way the county commissioners came around was that we said what we believed and what we intended and I think we became respected for that. We said that the county had been torn apart by zoning fights. The zoning fights are because people who acquired places to live in Howard County (were) disturbed that the area near them (was) going to be very different from what they anticipated."

The commissioners granted the zoning, the planners devised a brilliant town map, and the people moved to Columbia, Rouse says, all for one reason.

"Fundamentally, people want to do what's right," he says.

*B*rave New World

The families that moved to Columbia were pioneers.

In the late 1960s, the whole country seemed to be in revolt — two-hundred thousand marched against the Vietnam War in New York City, hundreds were killed in race riots in Washington, D.C., and Newark and Detroit, and thousands gathered in Haight-Asbury Park to take drugs and celebrate free love.

But around the country, some families heard a call from a city that claimed it celebrated harmony and integration and community. They visited the new Exhibit Center, staffed by both black and white hostesses, and watched slide shows of people of all colors and backgrounds intermingling in a city planned to give them a better quality of life. And they were charmed, lured by an idealistic Pied Piper to his new town.

One of James Rouse's four goals for the new city was "to provide for the life and growth of man, woman and family."

In 1968, John and Anne McGonigal returned to the United States from two years of service in the Peace Corps. They had met and were married in a village in Colombia — South America. In 1970, they moved to Columbia — North America.

"We already had two children, and we thought it would be a good place to raise them," John says. "And we were Peace Corps volunteers. We considered ourselves to be on the liberal side of center. It was important that our kids grow up in an integrated neighborhood and go to integrated schools. And it was very important to get to know our neighbors. We didn't want just a place you drive your car to and from. Columbia was what we wanted. It was a community; people were accepted no matter their racial mixture, or where they stood on the political spectrum."

Columbia quickly acquired its own icons — symbols that embodied the town's philosophy. A sculpture known as "The People Tree" was planted on the lakefront in downtown Columbia. Baltimore sculptor Pierre duFayet cast the fourteen-foot tree with sixty-six gilded people as branches. And Mort Hoppenfeld, the chief architect for The Rouse Company and the man who designed the fountain on the plaza near "The People Tree", coined the phrase "The Next America" to describe Columbia.

That phrase set goals, Rouse explains. Columbia would become a city of hope and truth, love and peace.

Now, more than a quarter-century later, Columbia's residents tell Rouse they love their

town. Often on his walks around Wilde Lake, or as he and his wife Patty are grocery shopping, someone tentatively approaches the bald patriarch to thank him for the city where they raised a family; Rouse feels he's done well with his town. It fulfills his "highest hopes," he says.

"I find I'm moved to tears about Columbia, about absolutely absurd things," Rouse says, and laughs a little bit, crinkling his eyes and raising his eyebrows, feathery as dove's wings. But this town wasn't meant to be an utopia, he says. It was merely meant to be a better city.

"The Columbia rationale in a nutshell was to build a rational city," Rouse says. "That emerges and gathers its importance from the fact that the American city was and still does grow by utterly reckless experience. Usually, somebody goes out and buys a piece of land and breaks it into lots and sells them, and then somebody else somewhere else, and then a lot of people pile up and then they have to build a road through it, and they have to knock down the front yards and the telephone poles and then they come and cloverleaf, and then comes offices and shopping. This is the wholly irrational way that cities grow. It made no sense.

"We raised the question — is that really the way cities should grow? Can't there be a rational development for the expansion of a city? ... Sprawl is anti-human. It's negative to the life and growth of man, woman and family. It was not constructive, it was not supportive. It was negative. It made life more difficult, not easier. It foreclosed the opportunities for nature, for convenience, for community. And thus was irrational, inhuman, anti-human."

People, Rouse decided, should govern the city; not the other way around. He had four goals for his new city; he recites them, apologizing that he sometimes mixes up the order in which they were originally presented.

"To build a real city, not just a better suburb, with all of the elements of a real city.

"To respect the land.

"To provide for the life and growth of man, woman and family.

"The fourth was to make a profit. You would be astonished how successful the fourth goal has been."

He pulls from his wallet a tattered scrap of paper—a fragment of The Rouse Company annual report celebrating Columbia's twenty-fifth year—and reads it aloud: "In the past six years, Columbia has produced earnings before depreciation in deferred taxes of $126 million. The current equity value of our Columbia land and income properties is now approximately $362 million."

Profit was important to Rouse. He wanted to show other developers that a human city can make money — as much or more than an inhuman one. And Columbia has been a success on the first three counts as well, he says.

"I think Columbia is a city. I think we have respected the land; I feel very proud of what we've done with the land. I think we've provided a better place for the life and growth of man, woman and child. I think there were a lot of subheads under that — to be economically diverse, to be ecumenical in the broadest sense of the word, to be racially open.

"We said we're not going to play God; we are going to be open, truly open. We opened (at the Exhibit Center) with ten hostesses, four black, six white," Rouse says. "When you went through the Exhibit Center, there were pictures of black and white mothers talking across the fence, black and white children playing together."

That slide show, Rouse says, sent a message that was "sincere and authentic." And black people got it.

Maggie Brown was one of them. She grew up in strictly segregated West Virginia. While working as a chemist in Washington, D.C., she met and then married her husband, Nesbitt. The Browns looked for housing in Silver Spring and Kensington, but nothing there was open to blacks. White realtors politely suggested that they probably "wouldn't be happy" in certain neighborhoods, Brown says. And when they finally moved to an established neighborhood in Baltimore, three-quarters of the white families on the block staked "for sale" signs on their lawns within the next year.

Finally, Nesbitt suggested they go look at Columbia. Maggie remembers thinking he was crazy, that people wouldn't live integrated like that.

"I was not quite the believer," Brown admits, laughing. Now, she is a vice president of the Columbia Association, the nonprofit group that manages and governs Columbia. But in 1969, she was a doubting Thomas. It was the pictures in the Exhibit Center that persuaded her.

On moving day, in July, 1970, they parked in front of their new home in Longfellow to unload their toddlers and plants and boxes. "It must have been ninety-nine degrees," Maggie recalls, and they were waiting for the realtor to arrive with the key. Across the street came a white woman, carrying a pitcher of lemonade and glasses. Maggie Brown says she was touched by the gesture. They were glasses, she says, not paper cups she was going to throw away after they drank. She thought then, and knows

now, "Maybe there's some truth here.

"Columbia gave me an opportunity to see people as they could really be at their greatest moments," she continues, "when we're trying to work together, when we're taking each other for worth, not because of how much money you make or your education or the color of your skin."

The Dream Realized

A pioneer like many others, Jim Rouse has made Columbia his home all these years. His house, an unprepossessing contemporary on the shores of Wilde Lake, looks like many of his neighbors'. From his windows, he can watch the steady traffic of pedestrians and bikers and joggers, along with the errant fisherman, around the lake. Though he no longer plays tennis on Columbia's courts, he walks daily with his wife around the neighborhood.

As the city has aged, celebrating its twenty-fifth birthday in 1987, so has its father. Jim Rouse is now eighty-one years old. He's had a heart bypass operation and a stroke; his steps are growing tottery. In 1972, he stepped down as chief executive officer of The Rouse Company to guard his health more closely, and to devote more energy to the Enterprise Foundation, a nonprofit development corporation he created to help restore inner-city neighborhoods.

Yet his conviction that planned cities — and his planned city of Columbia specifically — are an improvement over unchecked suburban sprawl remains undiminished. Some eighty-thousand residents now make their homes in Columbia's ten villages. The last, River Hill, is underway at the western edge of the city, where new houses seem to crop up practically daily.

To Rouse, the city seems both a miracle, and the predictable outcome of some of the most revolutionary urban planning of its time. Though it has its detractors — who claim that its unambitious architecture, its lack of public transportation, its still relatively humble downtown area fly in the face of successful conventional cities with their exciting and vibrant mix of uses and scale — Columbia has grown and prospered.

Columbia was built from ground zero. This phenomenal physical achievement now comprises thirty-thousand homes and two-thousand five-hundred businesses, one-hundred thirty-eight miles of paved road and seventy miles of bike paths, one-hundred forty 'tot lots' and three-thousand, six-hundred acres of 'open space.' But Columbia's greatest achievement, in Rouse's mind, is more ephemeral, more about the spirit of this place. He's most proud of the city's creation of a measure of racial and social harmony that was unheard of in the United States in the mid-1960s, and still seems impossible in much of this country today.

Rouse has heard Maggie Brown tell the story of her first day in Columbia many times. He repeats it, in fact, at some of his many speaking engagements.

"That's such a wonderful picture," he says of the woman walking across the street with a simple, symbolic offering — just a glass of lemonade — to welcome the Brown family.

"Maggie loves to tell that story. She never forgot it. ... That's what makes me cry about Columbia," Rouse says.

And then he does.

Columbia's young athletes choose from a variety of sports leagues; their parents and siblings are eager spectators.

The villages were planned so "that it was easy and automatic and comfortable to see one another and know one another, share hopes and fears and ideas and be able to deal with life together."

James Rouse

Columbia's physical foundation, evidenced in touches like mailboxes clustered on the corner of cul-de-sacs, was designed to increase the opportunities for residents to meet each other.

THE PLAN

What began as a marriage of convenience has turned into a love story. Twenty-five miles north of Washington, D.C., and nineteen miles south of Baltimore, Columbia was carved from a rural oasis amidst sprawling bedroom communities and traffic jams. The New Town was to be a better alternative — green, rational and convenient. In each of Columbia's ten villages, planners placed centralized shopping centers, schools, playgrounds, pools, a neighborhood information center and office space.

Integration, not only of races and religions, but of the places in which people live, work, shop, worship, and play, made for a user-friendly city. Columbians don't sit in traffic light after traffic light on the way to the library. Most children walk to school. Senior citizens trundle home their groceries in carts from markets near retirement communities. And families ride bikes to the neighborhood pools.

The villages were planned so "that it was easy and automatic and comfortable to see one another and know one another, share hopes and fears and ideas and be able to deal with life together," founder James Rouse explains.

The town grew by increment. Clusters of streets form developments, and clusters of developments make up neighborhoods, which in turn form villages.

A group of small villages, Rouse surmised, would encourage better relations among both neighbors and nature. Homes sit on cul-de-sacs that circle streams, fields and pockets of woods, in an effort to preserve existing topography. About five-thousand acres of Columbia are committed to open space — either developed as parkland and pathways or allowed to remain as forest. Almost three thousand of those acres are now maintained by the Columbia Association.

In a legendary story, one conservation activist managed to save a huge chunk of forest along the Patuxent River by persuading Jim Rouse, wearing his signature plaid jacket, to lie in a ditch and be charmed by the mating dances of the woodcocks in the nearby brush. Like the birds' breeding ground, many old trees were dodged by bulldozers or replanted elsewhere. And, to add to the bucolic air of the town, electric and telephone lines were buried, so poles wouldn't clutter the vistas.

Within the neighborhoods, Mort Hoppenfeld, The Rouse Company's chief

Residential streets were planned as cul-de-sacs and dead-end streets to reduce traffic in residential neighborhoods and increase the amount of communal open space.

architect, massaged the image of the town's aesthetic, hoping to offer a measure of originality, but also a sort of harmony. The result is a kind of uniformity that some have characterized as bland, but others champion as pleasantly balanced.

"We realized we were opening ourselves to the current state of the art of residential and commercial design in America, and that is not very high. It's a mixed bag. We have some of the finest, but more of the worst. The task was to make out of this open-ended mixture something harmonious and satisfying to live with," wrote Hoppenfeld, who died in 1985. "The only constant is quality," he declared. And that was the edict handed down to Columbia's homebuilders.

Jim Ryan, the thirty-four-year-old son of a Pittsburgh family of builders, arrived in Columbia in 1967 to build his nationwide Ryland homes business on the foundation of Columbia. Ryland, with its traditional boxy houses with three bedrooms, constructed more than fifty percent of the single-family homes in Columbia. The average home — from foundation to painting — was finished in just seventy-one days.

"Jim Rouse developed this town, with all these amenities; we just put the most house on his lots," Ryan recalls.

Many of the homes in River Hill, Columbia's newest and final village, border on protected woods and wetlands.

Previous pages 38-39:
Residents in each village
establish their own
homeowners' covenants,
designed to ensure
upkeep and provide
architectural restraint.

Village centers, located in the heart of the ten communities, provide a natural gathering place.

Debunking housing myths

Besides single-family homes, Columbia was infused with shots of high density — apartment complexes and townhouses — so residents of different economic circumstances would live enmeshed, eliminating obviously impoverished neighborhoods.

The Rouse Company set a goal of ten percent low-to-moderate-income housing units in the Next America, and placed those complexes in prime spots, near water or atop hills. And though the average household income of Columbia has now climbed to $72,150, Columbia still has no "wrong side of the tracks," thanks to the careful mingling of socio-economic groups.

"Initially when we laid out every neighborhood, we laid it out deliberately so that it would produce vertical economic circumstances," Rouse explains. "In Bryant Woods, for example, where I live, the lowest-priced lot sold for $4,500. The highest priced lots were those on the lake and sold for $15,000. We also had subsidized housing. This was very deliberately in opposition to the popular myth that you can't mix people by income level. It was also in contradiction to the popular myth that you can't mix people racially. ... People are really ready for so much more than we offer in the world. People live behind enclosures that really don't express what they want, in all kinds of ways."

More than three-hundred federally subsidized units were built into the original plan for Columbia, so low- and moderate-income families could afford to buy into the New Town. Churches and synagogues joined to form an interfaith charity organization and built some of the low-income and senior housing; in 1970, one month's rent for a one-bedroom apartment, including utilities, was $98. The federal government now subsidizes some apartments and townhouses, and for-profit developers have built affordable housing into their communities.

Other organizations, both for-profit and nonprofit, have established group housing for low-income residents, seniors, physically and mentally disabled people and emotionally disturbed youth, all within established neighborhoods.

H armonic convergence

While the planners included housing for those of various means, they also wanted to maintain uniformity.

Homeowners' covenants, the guidelines established by village residents to ensure property upkeep and architectural restraint, spare no one. Enforced through the civil courts if flagrant abuses are spotted, the covenants are created by elected village representatives and regu-

Connecting all the neighborhoods in the city is a meandering network of seventy miles of bike trails and foot paths.

Street names are derived both from local history and American authors like Faulkner and Dickinson.

late deck railings, fences, shutters and, as Jim Rouse discovered, paint colors.

When Columbia's founder painted his door a sunny yellow, he received a letter from the covenant advisor, explaining that his was not an approved color.

"My face is red because my door is yellow," he wrote back, and repainted his door.

Some murmur that the town's covenants add an element of Orwell's Big Brother, and that some neighborhoods are patrolled more vigilantly than others. But Chuck Bubeck, who moved to Columbia as a kid in 1967 and has bought two of his own houses in this town since then, says he never felt that the covenants were too restrictive.

"I feel they protect us," Bubeck says, adding that he has made many changes to his homes over

*Previous pages, 42-43: Every spring, garage sales continue
the annual circulation of Columbians' possessions.*

the years. Besides, he continues, it's not The Rouse Company deciding what is acceptable any more: "It's your neighbors. This is a democracy."

When Columbians speak to national catalog order companies, or correspond with distant friends, it's not the covenants that are amusing. It's the addresses. Friends chuckle; puzzled operators double-check the spelling. The Rouse Company's first development director, Kay Sarfaty, set the standard and chose each neighborhood's street names from the works of American authors like Henry Wadsworth Longfellow, William Cullen Bryant, Ernest Hemingway, J.R.R. Tolkein, Emily Dickinson, Robert Frost, William Faulkner. Subsequent Rouse employees followed suit.

Giving directions in Columbia is complicated, not only by the chambered nautilus design of the villages, but because of the incongruous street names. For instance, The Bowl is just off Camelback Lane. Mellenbrook Road leads past Logchain Road to Wild Bees Lane. And take a left onto Snuff Box Terrace from Cardinal Lane.

But all roads converge at the neighborhood's focus, where schools and playing fields, a neighborhood center for classes, meetings and day care, and the shopping center are clustered. Each shopping center contains a grocery store, plus necessities like newsstands, dry cleaners, video stores, pubs, banks, and liquor stores.

While combining facilities to meet the working, shopping and living needs of residents seemed rational, some thought integration of the races was more foolhardy. Conceived in the early '60s as race riots erupted in cities across the country, the Next America promised a rarity — fully integrated schools and neighborhoods.

When Rouse announced plans for his city in 1964, no one in the auditorium of the Ellicott City High School asked about integration. It simply wasn't pondered. After the meeting, a Baltimore Sun reporter questioned Rouse about open housing. The developer, warning the reporter that integration shouldn't be the focus of his story, explained that Columbia would welcome residents of any color. The next day's headline trumpeted that an "open community" was coming to Howard County.

But the idea of open housing lured hopeful people seeking an integrated community. About fifteen percent of the first twelve-thousand residents of Columbia were black. In 1990, according to the U.S. Census, more than twenty percent of Columbia residents were people of color — Asian, Hispanic or black. In fact, Columbians seem so proud of their racially and ethnically diverse community that they enjoy ticking off on their fingers the different colors of their neighbors.

Padraic Kennedy, a resident of Running Brook and president of the Columbia Association, recites, "On our street, there's African-American, African-American, African-American, white, Jim Rouse, African-American, Jewish, Ecuadorean, and — he won't mind me saying this — a Republican, Finn, Mexican-American. And that's typical."

Typical for Columbia, that is.

Almost as distinctive as its racial mix, Columbia's system of government is an anomaly. In 1982, Howard Research and Development Corporation, the land development arm of The Rouse Company, turned over governance of Columbia to the Columbia Park and Recreation Association, known as CA or Columbia Association.

Funded by a lien collected on homeowners, seventy-three cents per hundred dollars of assessed property value, CA is the quasi-governmental umbrella organization for various levels of nonprofit, incorporated community associations. Each development has a homeowner's association, each neighborhood has a representative on the village board, each village elects a representative to the Columbia Council, which acts as Columbia Association's board of directors.

The council, which controls a budget that in 1994 topped $33 million, was initially run by The Rouse Company. Gradually, as more residents moved in, control of the Columbia Council was turned over to its citizens, and the government was decentralized to the individual villages. A fledgling movement is afoot now to incorporate the city; the Columbia Municipal League was formed to back the concept.

T he end result

*T*hough each aspect of Columbia was planned, certain loopholes have emerged. The glowing vision of a speedy mini-bus system to whisk residents all around town has become the black sheep of the family — unwanted, unprofitable and underused. Teens and singles complain of an exceedingly family-oriented town with little for them to do.

But when a city is planned so carefully, the unexpected gaps become news. The most amusing occurred when The Rouse Company realized in 1967 that it had forgotten mortality. In a town planned down to the minutiae of school classroom size, number of benches along walking paths and allowable colors of shingle, Columbia didn't have a cemetery until 1989 when the Columbia Memorial Park, with a capacity for fifty-thousand plots, opened on Route 108.

And even death can't excuse the new town's late residents from covenants. The bucolic cemetery accepts no ornament taller than three feet. Bronze plaques dot the leaves of grass. No urns. Tasteful landscaping. Modest granite benches. It's tasteful —the Next America's way to rest in peace.

*I*t's pouring outside Bryant Woods Elementary School, but the first-graders can glimpse only slices of the gray sky and puddled pavement through the slim windows of their classrooms.

Fifteen children, their heads covered in blonde hair, braids, tight curls, crew cuts, are huddled at Donna Mitchell's feet as she demonstrates how to print an "f" on the blackboard. "Top to bottom, left to right, touching all the lines," Mitchell chants, as she draws the letter. Some of the children mouth her words, following her fingers with their eyes.

About ten feet away, past a desktop crammed with lunch bags and boxes, Melissa Forth explains capital letters. Her students sit with pencils at the ready.

And across the room in a darkened classroom, Denise Terkeltaub conjures up visions of steamy jungles as the water streams down the window panes; her children will soon be settling down to write a story about rain forests.

Many children in Columbia experience their first formal education in the city's many day care centers.

A new model

Bryant Woods, the first school to open in Columbia, still uses the open classroom model of teaching. Considered experimental when it pioneered here in the '60s, the idea of team teaching in large, semi-divided classrooms has become standard practice in elementary schools in Howard County, and many of the newer schools in America.

Innovative education was elemental in Columbia. From the beginning, founder James Rouse envisioned small, neighborhood schools where children would grow more intimate with classmates and teachers, and where teenagers would have more opportunities for leadership.

To make that philosophy concrete, The Rouse Company donated all school sites. And while the high schools eventually intertwined county and Columbia students, many of the middle and elementary schools have remained neighborhood centers.

Before Columbia, Howard County spent $380 per student — no kindergarten, no art, no foreign language in the elementary schools. In 1994, the county budgeted $6,054 per student — with on-line computer services, vocational training, French and sign language in the elementary grades, county-wide choirs and orchestras.

Columbia University Teacher's College has deemed the county's school system "one of the best in the country." High school students score consistently high on standardized tests, the system boasts the lowest dropout rate in the state, and eighty-one percent of its students continue on to secondary education.

And open space was integral to that highly rated system. With that model, Columbia's schools said goodbye to the old standards — classrooms with one teacher, one blackboard, thirty-five students and five flip-out windows.

Advocates for the system claimed that in the open space model, teachers could best use their particular talents. Slow and fast learners would be equally accommodated, educators said, and kids with different learning abilities could interact.

Over time, however, the glowing reviews of open space education have been modified. Fred Schoenbrodt, who served on the county's board of education from 1962 to 1978, and then spent another ten years on the state's board, supports open space classrooms, but with some alterations.

While the philosophy doesn't work as well in a high school setting because of the lecture style of teaching, Schoenbrodt suggests, elementary and middle school students thrive in the open space class.

"It permits parental involvement," he explains. "And little kids can't sit still for forty minutes in enclosed spaces. It keeps youngsters involved, it brought in teachers' aides. And it provides a homogenous group in a heterogeneous setting. Slower students get extra attention in smaller groups."

*R*iding the wave

If open space was considered experimental for its time, Wilde Lake High School could legitimately be called radical. Under its motto, "The school that makes waves," Wilde Lake allowed students to design their own curriculum and study independently.

One of the nation's thirty-six model schools, Wilde Lake has received mixed reviews over the years. More than traditional schools, argue some, the school's no-fail grading system and wide-open spaces opened cracks into which weaker students sometimes slipped. Mike and Louise Riemer moved to Columbia in 1969 from Cleveland. Each of their four children attended Columbia schools. "Two thrived on the open space, two didn't," Louise Riemer says.

Even those who appreciated Wilde Lake's unusual methods had reservations about them. Scott Kramer, whose family moved to Columbia in 1968, spent his last three years of high school at Wilde Lake. Now, he says, he wishes he'd had one more year to apply himself — he had just about got the hang of that independent study stuff, he laughs. Kramer ran Wilde Lake's photography darkroom, played instruments, and helped out with a school and community production of "Oliver."

"I was proud of it," Kramer says of his school. "I knew it was special. I knew the teachers were all hand-picked. We had a really special opportunity to really do something exciting."

Many Wilde Lake students say they discovered talents in themselves which might never have emerged in a more traditional environment. Deborah Jeffreys Hurley, who worked in theater and dance at Wilde Lake and now runs a video production company, explains that "the way we were encouraged and supported to explore our

Previous pages, 50-51: After the first-day jitters subside, she will benefit from a public school system widely regarded as one of the best in the country.

Howard County's school system, which spent more than $6,000 per pupil in the 1994-'95 academic year, offers students abundant resources and technology.

creative side gave us the feeling that anything was possible."

In 1994, the physical incarnation of Wilde Lake met the wrecking ball. Students now attend Wilde Lake at River Hill, a new school built for a burgeoning western county population, as well as the future population of River Hill, the city's last village. Wilde Lake High School will be rebuilt on the same spot by fall, 1996. The school will no longer be as open space as it once was, with its doughnut shape and two-floor media center. But the school will house the county's finest performance auditorium, which will be reserved thirty days a year for community use, a partnership that is another national first. The theater will be named after James Rouse.

B *eautiful dreamers*
The spirit of possibility that permeated Columbia's early schools also led to the city's innovative approaches to secondary education.

The city's planners wanted Columbia to have a university, and in 1968, The

Previous pages, 54-55: Planners established small schools in neighborhoods so that most of Columbia's children live within walking distance of the classroom.

Families continue their learning at Howard County's libraries. The system's circulation rate ranks among the nation's top ten.

Rouse Company and Antioch College, a liberal arts school in Yellow Springs, Ohio, started to raise money for a campus in Columbia. It was to be a work-study, field-based college with the ideals of pluralism and idealism at the core. Students would participate in the administration and management.

In September, 1969, the college opened in Oakland manor house with eighty-two students taking courses in environmental engineering, African-American studies, philosophy, and documentary filmmaking.

When Antioch moved to the Visual Arts Center in Long Reach in 1971, Dag Hammerskjold College took its place in Oakland. Named after Nobel Peace Prize winner and Secretary General of the United Nations, Dag Hammerskjold College aimed to educate the next generation about the world as a "global village" and to prepare Americans for rapid cultural change. Its students arrived from Sweden, Kenya, Israel, the Soviet Union, and India. But the college lasted only about eighteen months before its structure crumbled and its students abandoned it.

Antioch and Dag Hammerskjold colleges "kept the spirit of innovation, of risk, of change, of openness to trying new things," says Helane Jeffreys, who attended the Hammerskjold lecture series that brought anthropologist Margaret Mead to Columbia.

And if Columbians were ready for radical, they demonstrated it when they showed up to cheer on the inflation of Antioch College's pneumatic campus in a clearing in Symphony Woods. A contingent of kazoos played "The Star-Spangled Banner" as the bubble swelled. The inflatable campus was one acre of billowing frosted vinyl, heated and inflated with air blown by generators. But in November, 1972, Mother Nature beat the bubble into submission with winds and rain. Students gathered the shreds of their inflatable campus, and Antioch College, too, faded into the woodwork.

Instead, satellite campuses from nearby colleges like Johns Hopkins, Loyola, and Towson State University pitched their tents in Columbia. The School for Traditional Acupuncture, a thriving college for those learning the Eastern art of needle pressure, was founded in 1981 and now teaches more than one hundred students a year.

But Howard Community College, formed with funding from the county government, is the largest unit of secondary education in the city. With five-thousand standard credit students and twelve-thousand continuing education students, Howard Community College offers fifty programs of study, a

Eighty-one percent of Columbia's high school graduates pursue some form of higher education.

business and technology training center for local managers and employees, the state's only bio-medical engineering program, plus a full complement of arts and humanities courses.

*H*igh profile

The town's emphasis on education reflects its residents, about seventy-five percent of whom are graduates of four-year colleges. More than one-third have post-graduate degrees.

And they don't stop with college. Every month, about one-hundred thirty-thousand books, tapes and videos are checked out from Columbia's two libraries. The library's circulation rates among the nation's top ten. With hundreds of children's storytimes, readings and book clubs, library programs draw thousands of people a year — so many that classes are often filled a few minutes after registration opens. Formerly small branches located in village centers, the two Columbia libraries now offer more than six-hundred fifty-thousand books, four hundred magazine and newspaper titles, plus access to on-line databases, CD-ROMs, Macintosh computers and software, and remote dial-in catalogs and periodical compilations.

And the social experimentation of Columbia itself has been a living classroom. Growing up playing with all different colors and origins of people engenders learning, says Maggie Brown, whose three children — Kevin, Angela and Michael — are now grown. But she remembers watching them walk to school holding the hands of children brown, black, white, yellow.

"When you're a little kid, you're left to discover those differences that have nothing to do with color and everything to do with soul and spirit," Brown says. Columbia allowed its youth "to associate with kids from all walks of life so that when they get in other parts of this world, they're able to jump that gap that separates people. Exposure makes it easier to handle differences."

Since 1989, Howard Community College has raised $675,000 for its scholarship fund with the Columbia Classic Grand Prix.

Columbia Association manages pools, tennis courts, health clubs, and golf courses, including Hobbit's Glen, which has played host to PGA events.

Previous pages, 60-61: Symphony Woods, which surrounds an outdoor amphitheater with a capacity of seventeen-thousand people, stands as a quiet oasis in Town Center. More than three-thousand six-hundred acres of Columbia are devoted to parks, playgrounds and naturalized open space.

Columbia wakes up early on Saturday.

By 9 a.m., the soccer fields are swarming with players, the lakes are ringed with runners, the bike paths are studded with kids on tricycles, the tennis courts and weight rooms and aerobics studios are full. Columbia is known as the land of overachievers; they never sit still.

A lengthy list of activities clamors for Columbia residents' leisure time, from judo classes and swimming pools, to wood-working and bird-watching groups, to professional choirs and dance troupes.

But the town's most accessible resource is the land itself — pockets of forest and field fitted between developments. Almost one-third of the city's acres are devoted to open space; five thousand of the fourteen-thousand acres will be parkland when Columbia is fully built.

"The open space in Columbia is a very highly valued legacy to this and future generations," says Padraic Kennedy, president of the Columbia Association. "And as land elsewhere gets eaten up and goes away, it will become even more important."

CA now maintains more than three-thousand acres — mowing grass and building picnic tables, repairing swings, resurfacing paths and planting tulips. The Columbia Association feeds the ducks, clears the algae from the three man-made lakes, prunes all the trees. For ten years, CA employees even ran the five-acre Columbia Petting Zoo — usually in hot pursuit of the deer and llamas which regularly leapt the fences and cavorted around the mall — where they sold animal feed to residents who let goats gobble kibble from their palms.

Though their zoological experiment ended, the Columbia Association's one-hundred eighty-five full-time and three-hundred eighty-six part-time employees are kept busy. CA's staff manages all the town's recreational facilities, including two health clubs — the Columbia Athletic Club and the Supreme Sports Club — complete with jacuzzis, racquet courts and rows of stationary bicycles wheeling busily to nowhere.

Organized Columbia Association activities include teens-only dances at The Other Barn in Oakland Mills.

More than one-thousand five-hundred times a day, someone walks into the Supreme Sports Club to heft a dumbbell or dive into the pool or lace on roller skates. And every winter, the Columbia Ice Rink attracts sixty-thousand recreational skaters. CA also manages thirty-one outdoor tennis courts, more than one-hundred forty tot lots with swings and sand boxes, an equestrian center, and two golf courses. And when summer arrives, more than four-hundred thousand swimmers visit the twenty-eight outdoor pools.

Columbia residents or workers employed full-time at Columbia businesses may buy reduced-price memberships to attend CA facilities; about thirty-thousand people are members. Memberships are pricey — a season's outdoor pool pass for four family members is currently $244 and a package for two people that allows admission to the full complement of facilities costs more than $750. CA offers sliding-scale fees for lower-income residents, plus an earn-a-membership program.

The 'I'm bored' excuse can't possibly work for Columbia's kids, either. The opportunities seem endless — pottery and painting classes at the Columbia Association Arts Center, nature camps, Boy and Girl Scouts, Four-H, baseball, football and basketball teams, puppet shows and story hours at the libraries, concert and theater series featuring children's performers.

Teens are more hard-pressed for activities that don't require cars or capital. Organized activities repel teens as a matter of course. But CA tries. Free after-school recreation centers offer billiards, cooking, pool, skating, midnight basketball.

They don't come in droves, but they come, nonetheless.

*F*ields of opportunity

While Columbia has many pastimes, its passion is soccer.

Every spring and fall, parents converge on soccer fields to watch their offspring sprint from end to end in pursuit of the trademark white and black ball. After games, the town's fast food restaurants are filled with triumphant or crestfallen players — their cleats clattering on the tiles as they celebrate or commiserate.

This town's obsession with a European sport is the work of Felix Rausch, a German who acted as soccer's Johnny Appleseed in Alabama and Georgia before moving to Columbia.

Without a doubt, soccer is Columbia's passion. Nearly four-thousand kids play on teams sponsored by the Soccer Association of Columbia.

Walking through Wilde Lake in 1970, Rausch noticed some kids kicking around a ball during a Columbia Association-sponsored 'soccer' clinic. With volleyball poles as goals and volleyballs as kicking targets, CA had gathered a handful of kids to learn the game. Rausch saw that here, at last, was fertile ground for a soccer town; he called a meeting of willing parents in his living room.

"Columbia was unique, like Europe, clean and well-kept," he says. "I thought, 'My God, what a beautiful incubator for soccer.' It's like Columbia; soccer is the most democratic sport in the world. Anybody can play, it costs very little money and kids get lots of exercise."

By spring, Rausch had formed the Soccer Association of Columbia. Villages fielded teams of kids, each wearing jerseys bearing their neighborhood's colors. Rausch lined the fields, refereed the games, coached the clinics.

Now almost four-thousand kids play on SAC teams; the Memorial Day soccer tournament lures two-hundred national teams here for a weekend-long soccer love fest.

The town's public and private galleries provide ample access to visual art.

A full palette

Columbia's residents are also fiends for the arts, and organizers respond with a vast array of events.

With $1,000 and the collective literary lights of Ellen Kennedy, Jean Moon, and Prudence Barry, the Howard County Poetry and Literature Society was launched in 1974 with a small poetry reading. Thanks to HoCoPoLitSo, Pulitzer Prize and American Book Award winners the likes of Saul Bellow, W.S. Merwin, Gloria Naylor, Larry McMurtry, Maxine Kumin, and Isaac Bashevis Singer have spoken their words in Columbia.

A faltering chamber music series adopted by Norman and Nancy Winkler was transformed into a stop on the tours of world-renowned musicians. Columbia resident Eva Anderson, a dancer and choreographer, has taken her dance troupes around the world and back to Columbia again. And in 1993, Howard Community College joined Actors Equity, and now hosts professional repertory shows in its experimental black-box and large traditional theaters.

The icing on Columbia's artistic cake was applied in 1989, the first year of the Columbia Festival of the Arts. Backed by powerful sponsors and attended in 1994 by more than twenty-thousand people, the festival recruits national talent like Pilobolus Dance Theatre, humorist Garrison Keillor, violinist Itzhak Perlman, and stage star Claire Bloom for ten days of culture overload.

Arts events like the festival, or community groups like the Soccer Association of Columbia, were conceived in the spirit of creation engendered when a town starts from scratch. Rather like college freshmen, residents were dropped into neighborhoods together; they created their own traditions as they went along.

The town boasts the Columbia Film Society's foreign art-house film series, as well as a local business-sponsored bike ride for charity which attracts more than one-thousand five-hundred adult and child riders every year. Runners have gathered in Wilde Lake for more than twenty years for a long, communal jog, then bagels and coffee at the deli. And every year, hundreds gather for the city's birthday celebration. The crowds hush when Jim Rouse cuts the massive cake.

W *alk on the wild side*
The town's most established (and disestablishment) ritual, however, is the Longfellow Fourth of July Parade.

Started in 1970 with a few kids on bikes and some tentative musicians, the parade has grown official, but never stodgy. Every Independence Day, the neighborhood gathers to celebrate its own form of freedom, showering ribbons on virtually everyone who enters.

Over the years, the parade has boasted a motley collection of floats like the "Save Water, Shower with a Friend" bathtub (complete with bathers), contingents of bathing-suit-clad swim team members, a 'drill team' of cut-ups brandishing electric drills, neighborhood kids with bikes decorated to the hilt, the requisite veterans and politicians, plus, most years, a float poking fun at that year's most inflammatory city issue.

The parade, always followed by a raucous softball game between neighborhood teams, is the New Town's own particular bow to patriotism — tongue-in-cheek, but sincere.

WORK

*J*oseph Murphy is walking past undoubtedly the cleanest spot in Columbia.
After scrubbing the bottoms of his black cowboy boots, donning a white gown, a hair net and extra-large white booties, Murphy strolls past futuristic-looking labs as he explains AlliedSignal's intense focus on purity.

Every six seconds, every atom of air in the labs is exchanged through ceiling and floor surface vents. Each joint in the lengthy plumbing system is scrubbed, then labeled by date and plumber to assure that the water used in the experiments is so pure that it doesn't even conduct electricity. The air in AlliedSignal's labs is so clean that only one particle, sized about two-thousand times smaller than one square millimeter, is allowed in one cubic foot of space.

All of this blinding white purity is to ensure zero contamination of the microelectronic chips AlliedSignal manufactures to control navigation, communications, geological survey, and flight systems for clients like the National Security Agency and Motorola. Inside the labs, workers wear masks, headgear, knee-high boots, and Gore-Tex white suits, as they scrub, etch, cook, test, and wire the crystal chips. AlliedSignal, which arrived in Columbia as Bendix Field Engineering in 1969, now employs almost nine-hundred people.

Columbia has traditionally attracted high-tech employers. The first business in Columbia, Hittman Associates, engineered nuclear power systems. Fred Hittman remembers hiring a helicopter to circle his board of directors over the farms and muddy construction sites that were the embryonic beginnings of an untested town.

"What if it flops?" the skeptical directors asked. Hittman says he didn't have an answer, but that The Rouse Company's incentive package was so good, he couldn't say no. And Hittman Associates grew to employ five-hundred people.

Today, Columbia's high quality of life appeals to employees and businesses alike, Hittman says. That's why his business, despite having its nuclear divisions taken over, continues to manufacture medical implants in Columbia. But even from the beginning, he adds, "It was a good environment. It was the kind of place that highly trained and educated people would tend to flock to."

Under photography-safe light, an AlliedSignal technician inspects a tiny microchip destined for a navigation or communication system.

Encouraging growth

The Rouse Company, Columbia's developer and mega-landlord, sets standards for this town's aesthetics of commerce — signs are discreet, berms hide warehouses, lights are dimmed. When The Rouse Company sought to tone down the signs and lights at the city's first gas station, officials had to go all the way to a Sunoco vice president to change the company's style. The Wilde Lake Sunoco, as gas stations go, ended up looking quite nice.

Businesses are clustered in Columbia's forty-three office, industrial, and research and development parks, with about twenty-one million square feet of space. Often an indicator of the strength of the local business community, the vacancy rates in office buildings, research and development space and industrial sites were calculated in March 1995 at twelve, fourteen and twenty-three percent, respectively. Those numbers measure a gradual recovery after the overbuilding and empty offices of the 1980s.

More than fifty-two thousand people are employed by Columbia's more than two-thousand four-hundred businesses, which include names like Apple Computer, Westinghouse, Ford, and State Farm.

And the fertile business cli-

Developed by The Rouse Company, The Mall in Columbia was one of James Rouse's first efforts at an enclosed shopping center. More than six-and-a-half million people shop at the two-hundred mall stores each year.

mate has lead to one of the lowest unemployment figures in the country. Partly because Howard County has added five-thousand new jobs in both 1993 and 1994, unemployment hovers around three percent, almost three percent below the national average. About eighty-five percent of Columbia's adults are employed. Of those people, thirty-eight percent

work in Howard County, thirty-one percent commute to Washington, D.C., or its suburbs, and eighteen percent drive to jobs in the Baltimore region.

The recession after the boom of the 1980s dealt blows to the entire country, and Howard County was not immune. The shocks of that recession are still reverberating — the loss of General Electric's appliance manufacturing facility, layoffs at defense contractors like W.R. Grace, a drop in housing construction. Overall, though, the local economy is reviving and evolving, says Dick Story, the head of Howard County's economic development office.

One of the fastest-growing segments of Columbia's commerce is high-tech industry, specifically biotechnological firms, Story says. Columbia offers proximity to nearby federal

Neighborhood residents should be able to walk to life's conveniences, the planners decided. So they planned village centers at the core of each area, with grocery stores, pubs, dry cleaners, banks. Those centers provided many local merchants the chance to launch their businesses.

agencies like the National Institutes of Health, the Federal Drug Administration, the National Institute of Standards and Technology, as well as Johns Hopkins University and the University of Maryland Medical System. And the city also supplies a highly educated work force and room for growth, Story says. Manufacturing and distribution are also growing, he adds.

In addition, Howard County hosts the second-largest cluster of international businesses in the country — with thirteen Japanese and twelve United Kingdom businesses, plus Icelandic Air, a French paint company and a Belgian food additive research center. Most of those companies are located in Columbia.

Shimadzu Scientific Instruments, Inc., is one of those growing foreign-owned firms. Based in Kyoto, Japan, Shimadzu's North American headquarters are contained in two unassuming brick buildings in the Kings Contrivance village. Inside, engineers build and test medical and scientific measurement equipment. And every year, almost two-thousand scientists who are Shimadzu's customers arrive for a week of training on those instruments, which can isolate a tiny portion of an amino acid, or test a drug's purity, or determine every element in a liquid.

And Columbia has been the ideal environment to nurture a business, says Tom McKillip, Shimadzu's sales and marketing vice president. The company owns the huge field next door, reserving it for future expansion.

"As we attempt to attract new businesses to the county, Columbia itself is a strong sell; it's clearly the nation's most successful planned community," Story explains.

Capitalism central

C At the center of this success is The Mall in Columbia, which has become the capitalistic hub of the city. Teenagers migrate to the cobbled walks on weekend nights; senior citizens out for their exercise stride the level, air-conditioned halls before the stores open in the morning; the Girl Scouts hold an annual sleep-over there; antiques and craft merchants, baseball card and art and poster dealers all use the mall's aisles to show their wares. And more than six-and-a-half million people shop at the two-hundred mall stores every year.

James Rouse was one of the country's first advocates of the enclosed shopping

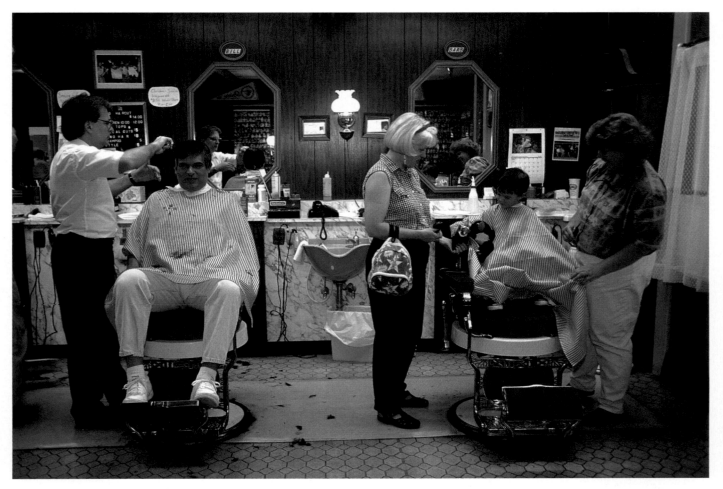

For nearly thirty years, fathers and sons have submitted to the scissors at Anthony Richard's barber shop in Wilde Lake Village Center.

mall. He started small, with Harundale and Mondawmin malls in the Baltimore area. The Rouse Company opened The Mall in Columbia in 1971, doubled its size in 1986, and plans another expansion by the year 2000.

Newer shopping centers like Snowden Square and Dobbin Center now house heavy-hitter discount stores like B.J.'s, Hechinger Home Project Center, and Kmart, which compete for customers with the small merchants in Columbia's village centers.

Those village centers provided many locally owned businesses their first start. In 1967, at age nineteen, Anthony Richard opened his barber and beauty shop in the Wilde Lake Village Center. As he has almost every Saturday morning since then, Tony turns on the tasteful red-and-white striped light outside the shop, then settles down for a day of taking a little off the top.

On the television in the corner, the weatherman is talking about the weekend clouds. A nearby wall displays photos of children having their first haircut. Tony is trimming around the ears of Sal Constantino, just like he's done every month for the last twenty years.

"He does a good job cutting off the gray," Constantino says. Tony harrumphs at the head before him, which has more salt than pepper atop it. "You want a little respect here," Constantino adds. "You get as little as possible."

Sharon Lee, in the "better half" of the shop, is eating her breakfast while she waits for a woman's color job to take. She was nineteen when she started twenty years ago. Now Lee styles hair for brides whose bangs she trimmed as toddlers. And she still drives over with her curlers and scissors to the Columbia homes of elderly clients when they're just not feeling up to snuff.

"As we attempt to attract new businesses to the county, Columbia itself is a strong sell; it's clearly the nation's most successful planned community."
Dick Story, head of Howard County's Office of Economic Development

he bulletin board at the Oakland Mills Meeting House is a melting pot of notices.
There are flyers for Parents Anonymous, the Jewish Festival, Lutheran College
Night, Catholic Charities' Adoption services, the Columbia Jewish Congregation's film series featuring "The Rise and Fall of the Borscht Belt," Inward Bound
workshops for Friends, an HIV-positive support group, and the Center to Prevent Hand-
gun Violence.

Alongside the colorful disorder of notices, worship services are neatly listed by
faith — Sabbath prayers on Friday nights and Saturday mornings, Baptist and Lutheran
services on Sundays, and Catholic Mass on Saturday nights, plus twice on Sundays.

The interfaith concept — by which congregations of different faiths would share
one large facility in order to make the most of building funds, parking lots, kitchens, nursery staff and offices — was part of The Rouse Company's original design for Columbia.

The proximity of one congregation to another, say some, has encouraged not just
physical closeness but also tolerance and sharing. Housed cheek-by-jowl, say priests,
rabbis, cantors, and lay pastors, they can take advantage of common facilities as well as
debate the issues common to their congregations, and those that differentiate them.

"You can dialogue out of a sense of identity, not a sense of weakness. You learn a
lot more about who you are by rubbing shoulders with those who are different," says
Father Richard Tillman, priest for St. Johns Roman Catholic Church in the Wilde Lake
and Oakland Mills interfaith centers.

Previous page: Interfaith centers were designed so congregations of different faiths could share physical space. What has resulted, some say, is a spiritual dialogue. Above: For 25 years, Columbians have gathered at Lake Kittamaqundi for an ecumenical Easter sunrise service.

*U**nder one roof*

When Columbia was being designed, The Rouse Company asked denominations to band together in the Columbia Cooperative Ministry, a group to guide the city's spirituality, and the Religious Facilities Corporation, which raised money from its congregations to build interfaith centers. On land bought at ninety-percent discount from The Rouse Company, the corporation built three interfaith centers in Columbia: Wilde Lake in 1970, The Meeting House in Oakland Mills in 1975, and the Owen Brown Interfaith Center in 1984. Faiths as diverse as Roman Catholic, Christian Science, Unitarian Universalist, Jewish, Lutheran, Methodist, and Baptist share the three spaces.

Columbians shared a "great burst of interfaith sentiment" when the New Town was being developed, says Rabbi Martin Siegel, the leader of the Columbia Jewish Congregation.

Father Tillman, who arrived in Columbia in 1977 from a traditional Catholic parish in South Baltimore, was slightly taken aback by all this interfaith enthusiasm. But he has learned to "appreciate the ecumenical interfaith nature of Columbia — hearing from and talking to my colleagues. I like being able to pass on the best parts of your tradition."

Like other congregations in the city, the Long Reach Church of God offers its young people structure and an environment of respect.

Though the interfaith concept was popular, at first, because it was symbolic of the spirit of harmony established in Columbia, it has not always had smooth sailing. A rough period, in which the interfaith centers became more a source of scheduling snafus than divine inspiration, followed the early days of enthusiasm. But now, say its supporters, the interfaith concept is growing again in importance.

"In the last couple years, the congregations have matured; survival is not in doubt," Siegel says. "The interfaith center has worked as a facility and on a personal level. Religiously, it has had its ups and downs. There was an idealistic beginning, then a down period. Now there's something of a coming together."

Tillman concurs.

"At times the symbol of cooperation is more important than the actuality," Tillman says.

"But the congregation wants to stay, regardless of what they have to trade off."

The congregations do interact: Columbia Jewish Congregation holds Bible awareness weeks; ecumenical Easter services have started at sunrise on Lake Kittamaqundi for twenty-five years; memorial services are often interfaith; congregations merge their choirs for Christmas concerts.

And the different faiths join forces to attend to social concerns. Siegel helped found the Clergy for Social Justice, an interfaith group which sponsors violent toy turn-ins, bus trips to peace marches, parenting workshops, and a cooperative effort with businesses and human service organizations to help the homeless. The Columbia Interfaith Housing Corporation was formed to pool money and build low-income housing and retirement homes for the elderly; it has evolved into the Columbia Housing Corporation.

But some congregations have chosen to break away from the interfaith centers. Individual congregations meet in elementary school auditoriums while saving money to one day build their own churches. And Beth Shalom, a Conservative Jewish congregation, moved in 1995 from The Owen Brown Interfaith Center to its own temple, the first free-standing synagogue in the county. Now, they no longer have to wheel the ark from storage every Sabbath. In their own worship home, Beth Shalom was seeking its identity, says Rabbi Kenneth Cohen.

Among classes offered by the Columbia Jewish Congregation is a course on bar and bat mitzvah preparation, taught by Rabbi Martin Siegel. In the interfaith spirit, the congregation also holds Bible awareness weeks.

*C*reating a community

In 1969, many of Columbia's Jews gathered to form a single congregation in their new town. They stopped going to temple in nearby Baltimore or Reisterstown, and decided to remain at home, worshipping how they wished.

"This was the '60s and '70s; we would sit around on the floor discussing what it meant to be a Jew," recalls Shep Jeffreys, one of the group's original cantors. The congregation assembled a looseleaf prayer book so they could combine ancient prayers and contemporary pieces about brotherhood, freedom, and peace. Teenagers played the guitar and flute during services.

"We created tradition," Jeffreys says.

Three years later, Rabbi Martin Siegel, "intrigued by the potential that Columbia represented," arrived. Shortly afterward, a rock band called the Electric Prunes helped divide an already dissolving congregation with its Yom Kippur performance of a solemn Hebrew prayer, and three separate congregations went their individual ways. The Conservatives split to become Temple Beth Shalom; the Reform became Temple Isaiah. The Columbia Jewish Congregation remained unaffiliated with the conventional Jewish designations and grew to encompass more than five-hundred families.

Columbia has nursed along other germinating congregations. The Rev. Robert Davis brought together five families in his Columbia living room in 1973. The Long Reach Church of God, as his congregation came to be known, met in Phelps Luck Elementary School and then for ten years at the Long Reach Village Center's Stonehouse. As its numbers swelled, the congregation sought its own house of worship, but could find no churches to found an interfaith center with them.

In 1978, the Columbia Religious Facilities Corporation sold a plot of land to the church, bending its rule to sell only to two or more congregations together. Now the only congregation to solely occupy what was to be an interfaith center, the Long Reach Church of God has expanded to encompass twenty-thousand square feet of church, Christian school and meeting rooms.

Similar to Baptist services in many more traditional African-American churches, Long Reach Church of God services begin with resounding gospel songs from the choir, pushing most to their feet. And one recent Sunday, just before a sermon admonishing parishioners to bear theological fruit to honor God, the Rev. Davis dunked twenty-seven men, women and children into a baptismal pool in the name of Jesus Christ. Columbia, Davis says, forged a spirit of creation, which helped nudge his church along.

The cross on the wall in Oliver's Carriage House, where the Kittamaqundi Community worships, was created from artifacts unearthed around the old stone building.

"Everybody was sort of starting out together," he recalls.

Now his congregation of one-thousand six-hundred families feels invested in the church they've created — with its youth ministry, its outreach to the poor and homeless, its door-to-door evangelism.

The sound of many voices

Perhaps because Columbians were pioneers and fond of creating their own traditions, they continue to be vocal about how their congregations should be run. At CJC, congregation members often lead and guide the worship: The rabbi is an "enabler," Siegel says.

Father Tillman agrees that Columbia residents feel more proprietary about their churches than in other parishes; his two-thousand six-hundred families contribute to the guidance of worship, and tailor it to fit their needs, he says.

"I think Columbia has a way of not allowing you to be comfortable in the fossil sense," he says. "I think it has a way of making the status quo not too static."

Jim Ryan, whose Ryland Homes business built about half of Columbia's single family homes, discovered that Columbia's dynamism altered not just his financial status, but his spiritual growth. After fifteen years of rubbing shoulders with Columbians of different faiths, he stepped down from Ryland in 1983 to become a pastoral counselor.

"Columbia really stretched me," Ryan says. "I was really religious when I came here. When I left, I was spiritual."

More than twenty-eight thousand times a year, counselors for Grassroots' twenty-four-hour crisis headline offer emergency services.

CONSCIENCE

A *group of teenagers with love beads clacking on their chests and bell-bottoms swirling* around their ankles lounged around a picnic table outside a Columbia office building to talk about the problems of their generation. For their new peer counseling program, Grassroots, they agreed on a phone number: 730-DRUG. The year was 1968.

"It was as hippie a group as you could ever imagine," laughs May Ruth Seidel about those Antioch College students.

When Seidel moved to Columbia in 1970, she volunteered with organizations like the League of Women Voters, the Urban Rural Transportation Authority and the Howard County Housing Alliance. But the generation of free love was still in full swing, and so Seidel also worked for Planned Parenthood, distributing sexual health information through Grassroots.

With the help of volunteers like Seidel, guidance from local psychologists, and funding from The Rouse Company and the Columbia Foundation, Grassroots has since evolved into a full-fledged crisis assistance center. The twenty-four-hour hotline receives more than twenty-eight thousand calls a year, all answered by trained volunteers and crisis counselors.

As the city of Columbia has grown, so have its problems. Most of the year, all twenty beds in Grassroots' emergency shelter are filled with homeless men, women, and children from Howard County and beyond, according to Andrea Ingram, Grassroots' executive director. In addition, Grassroots' twelve-bed transitional shelter, and the motel rooms it rents in emergencies, are usually occupied.

And virtually every day, a church, service club, or neighborhood group cooks and serves hot meals to the residents, or totes over a bag of toiletries or toys. Columbia residents are nothing if not willing; this city's cadre of volunteers is faithful and productive.

The Columbia Volunteer Corps, run by the Columbia Association since 1991, recruits about two-hundred new volunteers per year. That roster of willing people is tapped by one-hundred fifty county organizations which mobilize to bolster the weak, comfort the sick, feed the hungry.

*P*ulling *together*

The heady, chaotic beginnings of Columbia sparked residents to launch institutions as their own solutions to society's woes.

"There was a powerful community-centered interest here," says Henry Seidel, who moved to Columbia to help start the Columbia Medical Plan.

"I don't think you came out here unless you cared," his wife, May Ruth, adds.

Helane Jeffreys, who moved here in 1968 and helped pioneer what is now the Wilde Lake Cooperative Nursery, agrees. "The opportunity for creating new institutions meant that we created the leadership," she says.

Maggie Brown, who organized the City Fair as a volunteer for more than a decade, knocked on doors to solicit for the hospital's building fund, collected quarters for the Longfellow El-

Diverse institutions have benefited from the philanthropy of Columbia Foundation donors; Winter Growth Adult Day Care Center receives grants to fund programs for frail elderly and the victims of Alzheimer's Disease.

ementary playground, and has donned a bright red bathing suit for spoof fund-raisers more times than she cares to admit.

"If anything needs to happen there's a sense that people will pull together to see that it will get done," Brown says.

Columbia lays claim to a diverse group of nonprofit organizations — including domestic and sexual assault shelters, advocates for those with disabilities, a counseling center with sliding-scale fees, career guidance groups, and even a support association to help the nonprofit organizations.

"Columbia has always had the capacity to have a committee of professionals about anything," city founder James Rouse says, and chuckles at this town's propensity to rally and organize and meet in committee about an issue until that problem shrieks its defeat.

Rouse started that compassionate snowball rolling. He founded the Columbia Foundation in 1969, and convinced the Columbia Bank to dedicate a portion of profits to the foundation. Hundreds of other town businesses and philanthropists have followed suit. By 1995, the foundation had given more than three million dollars to institutions as diverse as Hospice Services of Howard County, the Children of Separation and Divorce Center, the Foreign-born Information and Referral Network and the Howard County Association for Retarded Citizens.

And the spirit of creation continues. Jean Toomer, who moved to Columbia in 1968 with her husband, Clarence, and her five children, was working in the Howard County Office of Human Rights in 1988 when a flurry of hate crimes inflamed Columbia. Toomer and a few others formed Community Building in Howard County "to bring people together, to identify similarities and recognize differences," Toomer says.

Now the organization offers multi-cultural arts evenings, sponsors the Mediation and Conflict Resolution Center with Howard Community College, and runs a peer mediation program in the county schools.

"Columbia presented opportunities to me; whatever the challenges were, I believed they were manageable," Toomer says. "And I believe they are manageable still."

*P*roblem solvers

Paul and Lynn Shoffeitt were eating out that night in 1971 with Tom and Margaret Ferguson at Karras' Beef House in Wilde Lake. While brainstorming about a different kind of counseling center, one in which psychologists would volunteer to provide low-cost mental health counseling, they suddenly looked at one another. "Why not?" they asked themselves.

On impulse, the group called Jim Rouse's office, found he was just leaving, and rushed over. They caught him in the lobby, and stood right there as they told him their idea. The next morning, Rouse cut a check for $10,000 to start the Family Life Center.

Now the largest provider of mental health services in the city, the Family Life Center has evolved as society's problems have changed. While it still offers standard one-on-one counseling on a sliding-fee scale, over the years the center has added such services as a support group for people who are HIV-positive, a social and mentoring club for African-American boys, and a networking and support group for unemployed people and their families.

The town's physical health has long been tended by the Columbia Medical Plan, a cutting-edge health clinic started in 1969, with Dr. Henry Seidel as its first director. Spawned from Johns Hopkins University Hospital and Connecticut General Life Insurance Co., the trend-setting plan offered residents low-cost, pre-paid preventive care — essentially, a health maintenance organization ahead of its time. Once premiums were paid, members could visit the plan, any time, for $2. As deficits spiraled and the number of patients grew, Blue Cross/Blue Shield bought the HMO in 1982. Its patients now number more than seventy-nine thousand, with more than one-hundred sixty board-certified health care providers.

"While the real goal of community participation in health maintenance is nowhere near achievement," says Dr. Seidel, whether here or in the rest of the country, Columbia Medical Plan brought in "an awful lot of really good doctors."

In less than three years, those doctors decided the town needed a hospital closer than Johns Hopkins. With just fifty-nine beds, Columbia Hospital and Clinics Foundation admitted its first patients in July, 1973.

After a proprietary tussle between county and the new town's residents, the foundation became a regional hospital a year later. And over the next twenty years, the hospital expanded four times. Now, Howard County General has two-hundred thirty-three beds. In 1994, its physicians performed eleven-thousand, three-hundred-ten operations. New health care additions to the city include a neonatal intensive care unit, state-of-the-art magnetic resonance imaging services in its own separate building, a regional oncology center and plans for an expanded surgical suite.

The hospital also administers to additions to the human race. In 1994, almost three-

The Wilde Lake Cooperative Nursery has been helping parents share the load of day care since 1968. The creative energy in Columbia sparked many residents to start their own institutions here, says Helane Jeffreys, one of the nursery's founders.

thousand women gave birth at Howard County General. Veteran labor and delivery nurses have now delivered Columbia babies in the 1970s, and those children's children in the 1990s.

On May 23, 1995, those nurses saw one more life breast into the world. After a six-hour labor (Dr. Julie Gould even had time to show Michael and Susan Firey her recent wedding pictures), Dylan Christopher Firey emerged in one of the hospital's birthing rooms. Born at 1:23 p.m., weighing seven pounds, thirteen ounces, Dylan increased Columbia's population by just one more.

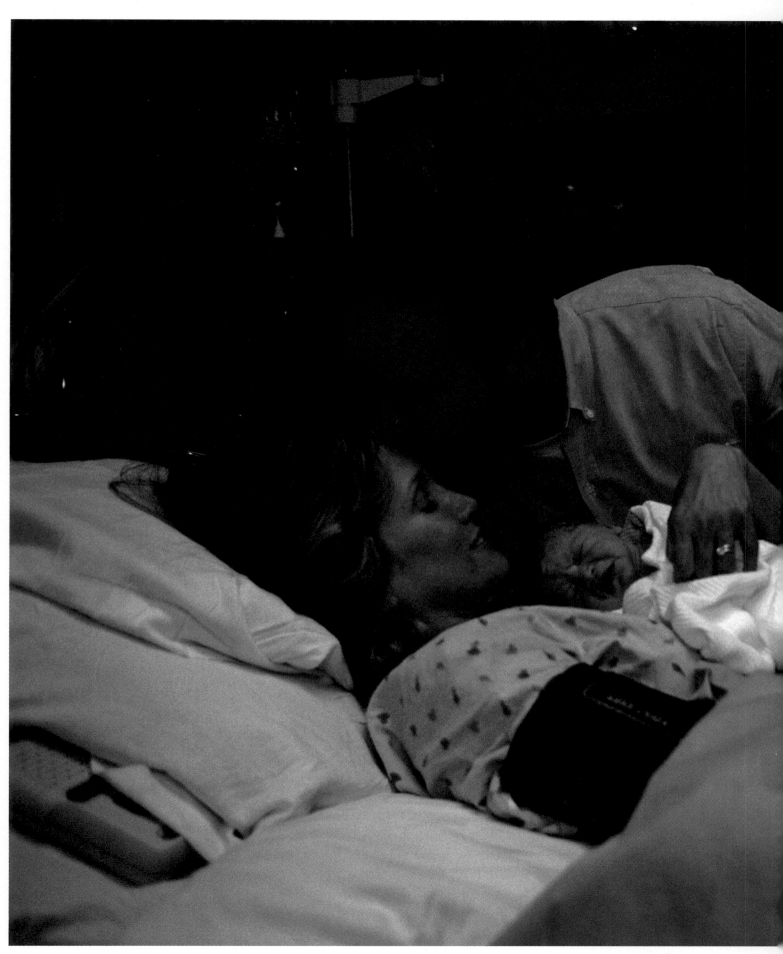

Moments after his birth at Howard County General Hospital, Dylan Christopher Firey wails while his father, Michael, comforts his mother, Susan.

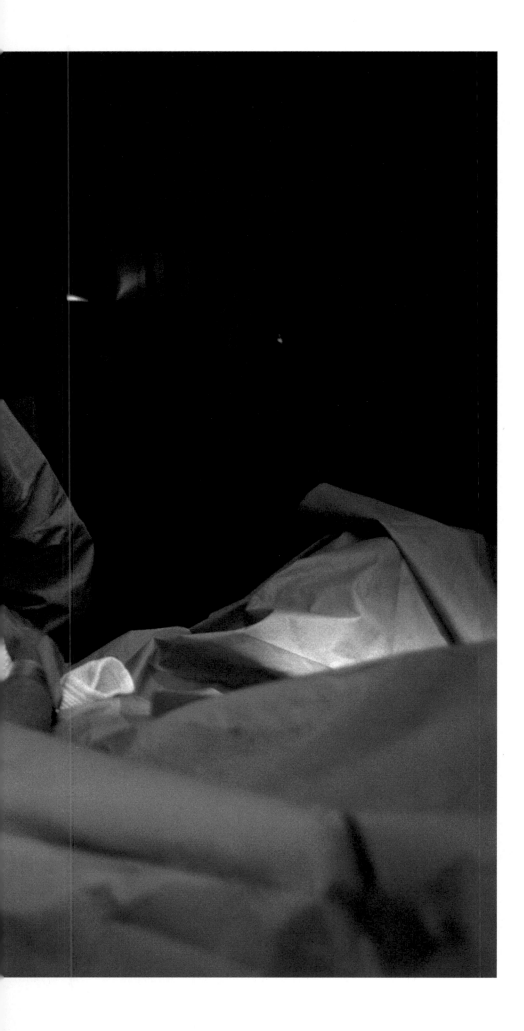

C When Jessie Newburn's parents decided to move from their Michigan neighborhood of stately white Victorians to the muddy cul-de-sacs of Columbia in 1971, the seven-year-old wasn't worried about leaving her friends or the towering trees or her room.

"I remember being excited," Newburn says. "I knew we were going to a new town, not just any place."

On April 1, 1971, the Newburns moved from Ann Arbor into their new home in Columbia's Thunder Hill neighborhood. Newburn remembers that her parents told her it was worth a higher mortgage to be able to raise their children in "a diverse and community-oriented place."

When she looks back on that explanation, it makes perfect sense to her. "I went from living in a school district with one black child to living next door to an African-American man," Newburn says now. "That opportunity to grow up with other kids of different backgrounds was a lesson I couldn't have learned as an adult."

City founder James Rouse once said that Columbia's ultimate victory would be to grow better people: "This is the purpose of our civilizations — the only valid purpose of any civilization, to grow better people; more creative, more productive, more inspired, a more loving population."

The second generation of Columbians, children who grew up in the city, have become adults themselves now, and they — perhaps even more than their own parents — believe in Rouse's words. They participated in Columbia's social experiment so fully that it is, for some, all the memory they possess. Many of those children have remained in their home town, marrying and raising families of their own, or have returned to Columbia after brief pilgrimages elsewhere. And some are now seeking to improve the city, to blow new life into its original spirit, and to alter its structure to suit a changing society.

"To have benefitted so significantly from a community environment and not to give back would not be living up to my responsibilities," Newburn says. "We moved to a town that was about growing people; that ethic was ingrained deeply."

Columbia's next generation, along with its founder and the rest of its residents, know the town isn't perfect.

Columbia's mass transportation system, while conceived as an efficient people-moving network, has not lived up to expectations.

The mass transportation system, ColumBUS, is inefficient and often short of passengers. The planned teen centers either failed to attract kids or spawned scuffles, and were drastically scaled back; that dearth has left youth with few opportunities for recreation beyond the thriving world of organized sports. Inflation and rising interest rates have made housing in Columbia expensive for single people and young families. Others claim that the architecture is sterile, the city too homogenous and middle class, the fledgling cultural movement too, well, fledgling.

Some citizens complain that the governance of the Columbia Association and the Columbia Council is distant and ineffective; the city should be incorporated and have a mayor, they say. The downtown area, most agree, should be developed more fully to draw people together in a place other than the shopping mall. Residents who may have forgotten or never known the original plan for integrating low-income housing into neighborhoods now protest its construction. Some say the city is too family-oriented, with little to offer singles and adults. And others, mostly the pioneers who moved here with high hopes, lament what they see as dwindling community spirit.

But Columbia was never meant to be a utopia, Rouse cautions, merely a better, more human, city. Columbia should inspire people to change their environment, to improve upon the plans made decades ago, he suggests.

"I felt that some people probably overstated, in their ebullience, what might happen, but I don't think they really expected the idyllic life and environment," Rouse says. "People did have disappointments. But I don't think they were many."

Columbia's original ideals and pioneering spirit have become diluted, many say, by people moving to the town for its practical amenities — neighborhood pools, good schools, health clubs —rather than for its social platforms of peace, love, and charity.

"Something of the original zest is gone," comments Henry Seidel, a physician who helped found the Columbia Medical Plan.

"People are moving here looking for a bedroom community," says Louise Riemer, president of the Columbia Forum, a group formed to offer suggestions on some of the town's problems. And community spirit is diminishing, she says. The Forum now hopes to

Columbia was never meant to be a utopia. The Next America has come to experience many of the problems faced by cities across the country.

"People are ready and waiting to do the job that is necessary to make their communities work. ... People are drawn by logic and reason and by a deep yearning for order, beauty and a good life. They will rise to the big, dramatically good plans — they will yawn at the timid, the cautious, the unconvincing."

James Rouse

"This is the purpose of our civilizations — the only valid purpose of any civilization, to grow better people; more creative, more productive, more inspired, a more loving population."
James Rouse

educate people about the town's original goals; it has resurrected an old tradition of sending neighborhood emissaries to welcome new residents, and hopes to encourage them to become involved in revising the city. Many residents either have forgotten, or never knew about the original, justice-driven ideals for Columbia, Riemer says.

But it falls to children to take up where their parents left off. And the second generation of Columbians remembers what Columbia meant to them while they were growing up.

Past and Future

Columbia kids remember spending hours dabbling in the creeks behind their homes; seeking their first measure of independence by taking ColumBUS to the mall; spending hours hurtling the fields in their soccer shinguards; nestling into throw cushions in Mrs. Z's restaurant as their parents listened to poetry readings; playing flashlight tag in the falling dusk with neighbors of all colors.

Casey Hickenbottom treasures the dozen friends he met in elementary school, boys who have grown now into a group of men. Sitting in The Pub in Wilde Lake with a beer at his elbow, Hickenbottom describes them by their ethnicities: "Three are Jewish, four are African-American, and the rest are white guys," he says.

Columbia, he says, allows people the freedom to bond with others based on their character, not their color. And his group of a dozen friends is still close enough to discuss the knotty problem of race relations, he says. For instance, one African-American friend has decided that he

Casey Hickenbottom, a product of Columbia's public schools, now teaches in the same system. He feels a responsibility for the next generation, he says.

was being "too white," Hickenbottom says, and is searching for friends with whom he has race in common. But he still talks about it with his old group of schoolmates.

"In Columbia, you can go in any circle you want. I've hung out with whites, blacks, Latinos, Asians," Hickenbottom says. "What it's shown me is that people are people, no matter what color. It has opened up a lot of different cultures."

Hickenbottom and his friends are successful — lawyers, entrepreneurs, physicists. They are highly educated. Columbia, Hickenbottom says, was an inspiring place to grow up, especially for people of color. "We saw people of all different colors doing anything they wanted to do."

Patty Bubeck moved to Columbia as a child in the early '70s. Now she is raising her children in the same kind of diverse neighborhood.

Patty Rodriguez Bubeck moved to Columbia in the early '70s. A Bolivian native, Bubeck says Columbia was good for minorities; here, she says, she grew up with opportunities. She later married a man who had moved to Columbia in 1967, Chuck Bubeck, who shares her ideals and those of Columbia. Now, they're glad their children, Patrick, Tim and Charles, can grow up with neighbors from different cultures; they learn about Islamic holidays, Jamaican food, Pakistani traditions. And that's just on their cul-de-sac, Patty laughs.

But Alice Cornelison, who wrote a doctoral dissertation on black youth in Columbia, cautions parents to warn their children about racism, which is less apparent in the Next America than in the rest of the nation. When Columbia kids emerged from their social experiment and went off to college or to work in other areas, many experienced severe culture shock — like deer blinded in the neon lights of the rest of the world. They call it the "bubble" effect. Sheltered in the slightly plastic world of the new town, they grew up removed from many of the world's problems: urban blight, segregation, poverty, racism.

"Columbia can make you kind of naive," Casey Hickenbottom agrees. "The real world's not like Columbia."

But as Columbia child Lei Hoffarth Ellingson quips, "Why settle for reality?"

Many of the second generation haven't settled for status quo. They're prepared to work for their community.

N*ew beginnings*
Columbia made it easier for Vince Guida Jr., whose family lived in one of Columbia's wealthiest neighborhoods, to make friends of different races and socioeconomic classes, he says. He and his friend Dan Forester walked from their large homes in Hobbit's Glen across the street to the apartments nearby to pick up Kofi Carpenter on the way to school. Now all three are working on their own camp for disadvantaged Columbia kids.

"Columbia's good, but it can be better," thought Vince Guida Jr. So he co-founded Each One, Reach One, a summer camp and mentoring program for at-risk kids.

"Columbia taught me to respect diversity, in ethnic and socioeconomic background," says Guida. "It made me feel like, Columbia's good, but it can be better. A lot of people are facing serious obstacles in Columbia. They need help."

Guida and Forester founded Each One Reach One, and Carpenter has joined up, in part as a response to the three young men's sense that Columbia is only as good as its residents make it.

Both Guida and Forester taught school for a few years, and realized how desperately some kids, those without stable homes or financial advantages, needed help. The public school system, the county's recreation and parks department, the Columbia Foundation and The Rouse Company backed them. They found the boys — twenty-five young men deemed 'at risk' by their schools — and in 1994 opened the first session of their camp.

The boys saw free movies, camped overnight, ate donated gourmet lunches, wrote in journals, worked in small groups on their goals for school and their family, learned about Martin Luther King and Mahatma Ghandi. The men tutor the kids during the school year, take them on field trips, call to chat, run a soccer team. During the summers, they specialize — Forester is a physical education teacher, so he coaches the soccer and lacrosse games. Carpenter helps them produce rap music. And Guida works with their schooling and self-esteem.

"I enjoy knowing that I made an impact," Guida says. "There's inequalities in this world. That's why the camp is called Each One Reach One. If everyone would reach out and pull someone else up with you ... ."

Casey Hickenbottom teaches third grade at Longfellow Elementary, a few miles from the elementary school he attended when his family moved to Columbia in 1967, because he feels responsible for, and close to, the children.

"I think when you're a kid, you have no bias. You're very open-minded. It takes a couple of incidents or it takes somebody telling you things that are not true to warp your reality," he says.

Hickenbottom works with the Black Student Achievement Program in the summers, acting as mentor, counselor and role model. "You can do these things," he tells his students, teaching them what Columbia taught him. Though he no longer lives in Columbia (the new town's night life, he laments, is sorely lacking for a single person), "I love it here," he says. "If I get married and have kids, I'd like to move back ... . People really don't seem to leave here, or if they do, they come back."

Chuck and Patty Bubeck never left. And many of Chuck's friends have returned to

Columbia "with a new appreciation," he says. When Chuck's employer, Apple Computers, wanted to transfer him to Atlanta, Patty sheepishly admits that she was so upset she locked herself in the closet. They didn't move. In fact, Patty's whole family is nearby — sisters, parents, grandmother.

"Columbia has given us a good, tranquil life," Patty says.

Jessie Newburn returned to Columbia after a couple years of bouncing around in California. Now she lives in an apartment close to the desktop publishing business she runs out of the Oakland Mills Village Center. Newburn also volunteers — tutoring students, publishing the Domestic Violence Center's newsletter, organizing and hosting benefits for Grassroots Crisis Shelter and the Sexual Assault Center.

"I have always felt a very strong mission about my life," Newburn says. "Columbia had a very special mission. I am one of the first people to be a true product of this town; I

"We moved to a town that was about growing people. That ethic is ingrained deeply," says Jessie Newburn, who returned home to Columbia to start her desktop publishing business.

moved here when the ideal was still fresh. Columbia's ideal is about making a community better. And while I've never had a nationwide, grand-scale project, I have often envisioned a small comprehensive project that empowered communities."

She now organizes clothing swaps, in which donated clothing is sold for $1 an item to raise money. That way, needy people find bargains, money is raised, and "affluent people understand that everything they consume has to go somewhere," she explains. The last swap she orchestrated raised $3,000 for the Domestic Violence Center. She sees her efforts as "reasonable, bite-sized ways to help the community."

Onward and Upward

ORouse once said, "People are ready and waiting to do the job that is necessary to make their communities work. ... People are drawn by logic and reason and by a deep yearning for order, beauty and a good life. They will rise to the big, dramatically good plans — they will yawn at the timid, the cautious, the unconvincing."

Many heard his clarion call, and they raised their children in the society he envisioned. Rouse and many other believers imagined a rational town as a sort of benevolent parent which would raise, in turn, an enlightened generation. Now, that generation is returning, and with it, some imagine, comes a fresh hope for the Next America.

Columbia's residents today face problems different from those tackled by pioneers who moved here in the socially turbulent 1960s. The new town is not likely to remain insulated from the crime, racism, poverty, recession, and violence that trouble other parts of the country.

But the second of this town's generations, and many of its first, are hopeful that today's problems are no more insurmountable than those faced by Rouse and his group of planners. In September, 1964, Rouse and the fourteen other planners authored a report on their work on this new city of Columbia — a chronicle of their hopes and dreams for a new American dream.

"One of the fundamental goals in the building of this new city is to establish a process which will provide a better social and physical environment in which its citizens can grow to a fuller expression of themselves," the report reads. "A community is, by definition, an organic process, and its real worth is in its human vitality and the loyalty and love held for it by its people."

A History of the "Next America"

David Hobby

Documenting the history of this town is rather like filling in a sprawling family tree. Odd anecdotes crop up among the concrete facts that historians prefer. But, like children who love to look at pictures of themselves as babies, this young town's residents are awfully fond of recounting their part in the creation of a city. What follows is a social timeline of a history-making town.

Historical photos courtesy the Columbia Archives, except where noted.

THE TIMELINE

1962
•Nov. 3 First land package purchased, 768 acres.

1963
•Jan. 31 Connecticut General commits $18 million for land acquisition, later increased to $23.5 million.

•Oct. 30 Columbia announced.

•November Work group meets to discuss the new city.

1964
•Nov. 11 Plans for the city presented to the three county commissioners and local press at the Ellicott City Junior High School. "The best of

1964: Planners, including James Rouse (third from right), debate the details of the new city.

town and country," Columbia is called. New town zoning ordinance recommended to county; plans displayed at Smith House on Route 29.

1965
Eleven Protestant denominations sign covenant establishing the Columbia Religious Facilities Corporation and Columbia Cooperative Ministry.

•Aug. 9 County grants revised plan's zoning

approval for 13,690 acres.

•October The National Symphony announces Merriweather Post Pavilion as its summer home.

•December Connecticut General announces $50 million funding for Columbia.

•Dec. 10 Columbia Association incorporated.

•Dec. 15 Management agreement between Columbia Association and Howard Research and Development.

1966
Under construction: Lake Kittamaqundi, with an island to protect pin oak trees; the Exhibit Center; The Cove; Bryant Gardens. Jack Slayton, the former city manager of Vancouver, is Columbia Associaton's first director. Fred Hittman decides to move his engineering firm to Oakland Ridge Industrial Park, making it Columbia's first business. The middle school concept is adopted by Board of Education. Columbia model displayed at Smith House on Route 29. Columbia Religious Facilities Corporation pledges $1.4 million for interfaith centers.

•January The county Board of Education asks for $2.5 million for Howard Community College.

•March Howard County endorses money for HCC.

•May Johns Hopkins announces its intentions to establish a satellite medical system here.

•June Construction begins on Wilde Lake. Site on Little Patuxent Parkway picked for HCC.

•July The 23-acre Wilde Lake is dug and filled.

•October Lake Kittamaqundi is completed.

1967
Openings: Wilde Lake; Bryant Woods and Faulkner Ridge pools; Wilde Lake Tennis Club; Bryant Woods Children's Center; the first model home (on William Tell Lane); Teacher's Building. Hochschild Kohn announces plans to open in the Mall in Columbia. Low- and middle-income

housing announced by the archdiocese of Baltimore and the Columbia Cooperative Ministry; they build apartments, townhouses, and Shalom Square for elderly.

•Jan. 3 A 132-acre site is approved for HCC.
•Jan. 16 Columbia Horse Center opens at original location on Route 108.
•May 12 Groundbreaking for Hittman Corporation.
•June 2 John Levering becomes CA's second manager after Jack Slayton's death.
•June 21 Dedication ceremony at Wilde Lake Dam, followed by a cocktail reception.
•June 22 Exhibit Center opens to public. A car tour route is established, with signs indicating future amenities. ColumBUS starts with a six-mile route. Fares are ten cents, thanks to a state grant.
•June 30 Hobbit's Glen Golf Course opens, after repairs are made to the greens when cows rampage the turf.
•July 1 First residents of Columbia move into their homes in Bryant Woods.
•July 14 Merriweather Post Pavilion opens with the National Symphony Orchestra playing "Columbia (Broadside for Orchestra on Columbia Themes)." Senator Ted Kennedy and Marjorie Merriweather Post attend.
•July 26 Columbia Bank and Trust opens in a trailer in Wilde Lake Village Center.
•July 29 Wilde Lake Village Center opens with Giant, Columbia Bank, and the Pharmacy, with the town's first restaurant, The Eagle's Nest, inside.
•Aug. 15 The first letter is mailed from Columbia, in a makeshift post office in the carriage house on Wilde Lake. It was addressed to President Johnson.
•Sept. 1 Columbia's first gas station, a Sunoco in Wilde Lake, opens.
•Sept. 13 Charles Russell, the first baby of Columbia, is born to Charles and Barbara

1968: Town Center and Wilde Lake begin to sprout from the farm fields of Howard County.

Russell, an interracial couple.
•Sept. 17 The first Protestant church service is held at Slayton House. The first Catholic Mass and ecumenical services closely follow.
•Oct. 1 The first residential lots in Harper's Choice are sold.
•Oct. 5 Slayton House, named for Jack Slayton, is dedicated.
•Oct. 8 First town meeting, conducted by James Rouse, John Levering, and Bill Finley, is held.

1968
PGA tournament at Hobbit's Glen. Peabody Conservatory starts classes at Oakland Manor. Construction grading begins in Oakland Mills. Debuts: The Columbia Choral Society; the Columbia Chess Club; dance and drama classes for kids at Slayton House; the Columbia Swim Team; "Satya Graha," (meaning truth/love and force), also known as the Columbia Youth Association, starts with dances, movies and folk singing; the first Columbia fire house; first recognized horse show; 200 mercury vapor lights installed along four miles of Columbia roads.

Statistics: 1,200 families, 18 industries, four restaurants and a 7-Eleven now call Columbia home.
•Jan. 17 Harper's Choice deed and agreement

signed.

•Feb. 5 The first issue of the Columbia Times appears in the Howard County Times.

•Feb. 11 Johns Hopkins announces plans for the Columbia Medical Plan.

•Feb. 19 First village elections, held for Wilde Lake, with Bill Crawford elected the first Columbia Council representative.

•Feb. 26 First Brownie troop established.

•March James Rouse starts up the Columbia Foundation, with his own money, plus an agreement from Columbia Bank to donate a portion of its profits every year.

•March 14-16 Work group reunion conference.

•April 1 Columbia sends food and supplies to help Baltimore riot victims.

•April 2 Wilde Lake Swim Center opens, but the canvas top blows off and heaters are ineffective.

•June First Columbia Antique Show held.

•August George Wallace plans to rally at Merriweather Post Pavilion in his presidential bid. Residents are up in arms and plan a counter-rally. They place a full-page ad in Washington Post touting the new town's tolerance and racial harmony, and inviting Wallace to experience brotherly love. Both the Wallace and the opposition rallies are poorly attended — a drenching rain storm keeps people home.

•September Head Sportswear, which manufactures tennis racquets, skis, and sportswear, opens. Bendix announces its intention to build a 143,000-square foot headquarters here.

•Sept. 6 Bryant Woods Elementary opens, the first new town school.

•Sept. 9 The Film Society forms.

•Oct. 28 The Wilde Lake library opens in the village center, with 8,000 books.

•November Omar Jones is elected Howard County's first executive, replacing the county commissioners.

•Nov. 7 Oakland Mills deed and covenant agreement signed.

•Dec. 21 First Columbia-wide Yule decorating contest held.

1969

Lakes freeze solid; CA supervises ice skating on Kittamaqundi. Columbia Association budget made public. Underpass parties are in vogue. The AAU Junior Olympics Diving Championship is held at the Swim Center. In the first flag football game, the Faulkner Ridge team beats the Columbia Colts.

Debuts: Columbia Youth Services; Theater Upstairs; the first cooperative nursery school, formed by Marian Grace, Helane Jeffries, and Bobbi Pilorio in Wilde Lake; Running Brook, Thunder Hill, and Swansfield pools and neighborhood center open.

•February Woodward and Lothrop announces plans to build in the Mall in Columbia, which is still a sweeping field of weeds. Johns Hopkins Medical Institutions and Connecticut General Life Insurance team up to offer the Columbia Medical Plan.

•May 17 Banneker Road fire station opens.

•June Hannibal Grove townhouses and apartments open; General Electric announces its appliance plant plans, with 12,000 potential employees; Garland Dinner Theatre, now known as Toby's, opens.

•June 18 First issue of the Columbia Flier appears, an eight-page shopper delivered free to 2,000 households.

•June 22 Wilde Lake Interfaith Center groundbreaking.

•June 25 Columbia's first twins are born, Wayne and Miles Ohlrich.

•September Antioch College of Yellow Springs, Ohio, opens a field-study college in Oakland Manor.

•Sept. 8 Second PGA golf tournament held at

Hobbit's Glen.

•October Johns Hopkins outpatient clinic opens in the Banneker Building.

•Oct. 11 The Chamber of Commerce and Columbia Jaycees begin meeting.

•November Oakland Mills Village Center dedicated.

•December The Rouse Company moves its headquarters here from the Village of Cross Keys.

•Dec. 19 Esso station opens on Little Patuxent Parkway.

1970

Statistics: Population is 8,798; 31 percent of the residents are younger than 10; 55 miles of sewers are laid, and 50 miles of roads. First village elections are held in Oakland Mills. Vigorous senior citizen Evelyn Haynes starts the Friendship Exchange to welcome new residents and help needy families. She brings food and wine, and offers an apartment to those whose houses are unfinished, or who are evicted.

Debuts: Thunder Hill, Longfellow, and Running Brook elementary schools; Talbott Springs pool and neighborhood center; Grassroots Crisis Intervention Center is started by Antioch College students and others; Eyre Bus Services begins shuttles to Washington.

Near debuts: Bendix's plan for elevated transportation system deemed too costly.

•Feb. 27 Tilbury Woods apartments catch fire.

•April 4 ITT Electro-Physics Laboratories groundbreaking on Route 108.

•May 7 Columbia Interfaith Housing dedicates its first low- and middle-income housing units.

•May 14 B&O and C&O railroads complete a four-and-a-half-mile railroad spur to the industrial area at Gateway.

•May 29 Mall surveying starts.

•June 12 Mall construction begins.

•July 4 The first Longfellow Fourth of July parade starts at Longfellow Elementary School and meanders around Hesperus Drive and Eliots Oak Road. A softball game with free beer and a no strike-out rule follows.

•September Howard Community College opens.

•Sept. 20 Wilde Lake Interfaith Center dedicated.

•Dec. 10 Zeke Orlinsky is the first community-elected director of Columbia Council.

1971

Statistics: Homes cost $50,000 in Hobbit's Glen; the family rate for Columbia Medical plan users jumps from $51 per month to $65 per month; pool membership is $35 per season; population is 17,000; the one-millionth visitor comes to the Exhibit Center.

Debuts: First rabbi, Israel Drazin; first girls softball league, Atholton Youth Recreation Association; Delta Sigma Theta chapter; Friends of the Howard County Library; New City Singers, Amateur Radio Club; the Women's Center; Steven's Forest pool; Tennis Barn. A bomb explodes at Wilde Lake Interfaith Center, injuring one man from Savage. Howard Research and Development gives Antioch College $12,000 to study wildlife and water quality in the Middle Patuxent valley.

•Jan. 26 Marriott proposes a theme park, "Great America," near Columbia.

•Feb. 13 Columbia Ice Rink opens in Oakland Mills.

•Feb. 27 Kahler Hall, named for Charles Kahler, opens.

•April Route 29 becomes four lanes. Anti-war rally held in downtown.

•May First appliances roll off assembly line at GE plant.

•May 2 Columbia Health Club, later the Colum-

bia Athletic Club, opens in Harper's Choice.
•June 14 Columbia tour bus ends.
•Aug. 2 The Mall in Columbia opens; 10,000 people shop on the first day. Original tenants include: McCrory's, Patowmack Toys, General Nutrition, Airport, Scan, Jade Palace, and Barry's.
•Sept. 7 Wilde Lake High School opens with 889 students.

1972

Columbia Association Executive Committee votes to oppose water tower in Harper's Choice. First bank robbery in town, at the First National in Oakland Mills. Private security guards patrolling commercial sections begin to carry guns.

Statistics: 23,000 residents, three zip codes (21044, 21045, 21046), 60 industries, 140 retail businesses, six banks.

Debuts: volunteer-run post office in Oakland Mills; first private physician's practice; Locust Park pool; National Organization for Women local chapter; Putt Putt Golf in Oakland Mills; first fast food — Jack in the Box in Wilde Lake

1972: Hurricane Agnes floods South Entrance Road. One woman drowns nearby.

and Dino's in Oakland Mills; 997 telephone exchange started because 730 has hit capacity; disputed water tower in Harper's Choice; Town Center and the Lakefront at Kittamaqundi are

built; Package Plan starts — cost is $200 per family or $125 per individual; women are admitted to Columbia Jaycees, despite national policy; Soccer Association of Columbia; first covenant advisor, Andy Savin; Family Life Center.

•January Loyola College starts classes in the American City Building. Padraic Kennedy hired as director of Columbia Association.
•Feb. 26 Cross Keys Inn, later the Columbia Inn, opens with 289 rooms.
•May Maryland Bicycle Racing Championships held here.
•June 21 Hurricane Agnes drowns one Columbia woman; 15 feet of water covers South Entrance Road.
•June First Ball in the Mall held to celebrate the fifth birthday of the town.
•September Johns Hopkins University starts evening classes.
•Sept. 20 Marriott's proposal to build nearby theme park is rejected.
•October Construction begins on Twin Cinemas, the town's first movie theater.
•Oct. 30 Dag Hammerskjold College opens.
•Nov. 22 Groundbreaking for Rouse Company building.

1973

Doug Du Vall hired as Wilde Lake High School football coach. Edna Hill, a 16-year-old from Oakland Mills, is selected the third Miss Black Teenage America (Dr. Hill is now a physician.) The first Columbia Association bonds are issued to finance facility building. Disturbances ensue at Merriweather Post Pavilion when groups like the Grateful Dead and others perform. Owen Brown land sold to builders.

Debuts: Columbia Figure Skating Club; Howard County FISH; Columbia Book Club (first book discussed, "I'm OK, You're OK"); Columbia

1973: Founding father James Rouse cuts the cake to celebrate his town's sixth birthday.

Natural Food Coop; Youth Employment Services; Phelps Luck pool; Child Development Center at Wilde Lake High School.

Statistics: Population: 30,000.

•May 22 Columbia Cinemas opens with "Hitler: The Last 10 Days."
•July 9 Columbia Medical Center, later known as Howard County General Hospital, admits its first patients.
•July 21 First patrons visit the llamas, goats, sheep, and deer at the Columbia Petting Zoo in Symphony Woods.
•December First poinsettia tree installed in the Mall in Columbia — 26 feet of red and white plants arranged in a cone. The tree has become a

tradition in the city.

1974

Statistics: 90 industries; more than 400 businesses; 17,000 jobs.
Owen Brown joins the Columbia Council.
Gas crisis forces two-hour waits at fuel stations.
Construction starts on the Oakland Mills Meeting House. A real estate slump leads to layoffs at Howard Research and Development and Rouse Company. Columbia Association slices its staff 75 percent and moves to Le Garage to save money. Howard Research and Development bans rock concerts at Merriweather Post Pavilion. The much-too-popular Call-A-Ride, a Columbia Association door-to-door shuttle service, ends from overuse.

Debuts: Visual Arts Center; CA's office for performing arts; the village of Dorsey's Search is added to Columbia's plans when HRD supplements New Town zoning with 747 acres; the Columbia satellite office of the Howard County Health Department.

•April 3 The Long Reach Village Center and Stonehouse open.
•April 16 Mrs. Z's, a restaurant on Cedar Lane which sponsored poetry readings and musical performances, opens with a light menu. A lending library and kids' corner are built into the restaurant that became Columbia's living room.
•June 17 The Rouse Company building opens on Lake Kittamaqundi.
•June 22 Columbia's third major body of water, Lake Elkhorn, a 39-acre man-made lake with a path around it, is completed.
•September Brunswick Bowling Center opens on Snowden River Parkway.
•November The Howard County Council elects its first slate of Columbia residents, including Ruth Keeton, Virginia Thomas, Dick Anderson,

and Lloyd Knowles.

•Nov. 19 The first Howard County Poetry and Literature Society programs held. Poet Carolyn Kizer and future Maryland Poet Laureate Lucille Clifton talk about their lives at a Women's Center event, then read to students at Wilde Lake High School. That night, the two prize-winning poets read their work at Wilde Lake Interfaith Center.

1975

A federal court rules that Karen Hendrixson may not try out for the boys soccer team at Wilde Lake High School. The first Vietnamese refugees settle here. A Harvard University study gives Columbia schools an A+. The first and last male go-go dancers grind away at Marmaduke's Moustache. GE lays off 500 workers.

Statistics: Population 38,000; 600 offices and retail stores; two million square feet of office space.

Debuts: the official Columbia Council with a representative from each village; the "no mow" policy on CA open space (instituted to save money and naturalize the areas); Clyde's restaurant on Lake Kittamaqundi; the Owen Brown Tennis Club; Dasher Green and Clemen's Crossing pools; the Memorial Day soccer tournament; Center for Traditional Acupuncture clinic; the first aerobics classes begin at the village centers; Hechts replaces the departing Hochschild Kohn in the Columbia Mall.

•May 18 The Oakland Mills Meeting House holds its first services.
•June Skateland opens to the delight of thousands of Columbia teens.

1976

The Young Columbians make a nationwide tour with a bicentennial show. Wilde Lake boys soccer team takes the Class B state title. Antioch College takes over the Visual Arts Center. Male and female streakers run through the Mall in Columbia with paper bags atop their heads. Cergy-Pontoise, a planned new town outside Paris, is declared Columbia's sister city.

Debuts: Howard County Association for Retarded Citizens' first group home; Jeffers Hill pool; Route 175 opens between Route 29 and Tamar Drive.

Statistics: Houses cost from $39,000 to $125,000 in Columbia; population 40,000; 37 builders; 108 model homes.

•January The Long Reach branch of the county library opens.
•April 16 King Carl Gustaf of Sweden visits Columbia — he is sung to by Bryant Woods' students, tours the mall, and is given two duck decoys and a gold People Tree pin.
•Nov. 24 More than 550 women attend "A Day for All Women," co-sponsored by the Women's Center and Howard County Poetry and Literature Society. Twenty workshops — from coping with death to getting in touch with the clown inside — preceed a reading by Judith Viorst.
•December HRD announces annexation of Dorsey's Search village; rezoning approved.

1977

CA treasurer Walter Davis embezzles $195,000 from CA; he is sentenced to jail for five years and never heard from again. GASP (Group Against Smoker's Pollution) lobbies the County Council for a smoking ban in public places. Kings Contrivance Village under construction. Cergy-Pontoise group visits Columbia. Marriott resubmits its proposal for a theme park nearby, but it is again rejected.

1977: Children representing each of Columbia's first ten years pose for a commemorative photo.

Debuts: sandwich smorgasbord Roy's Place Too; Skipjack's; Magic Pan; the first funeral home, Russell C. Witzke, opens; Package Plan II inaugurated.

Statistics: 45,000 residents (3.2 occupants per household); 20,000 jobs.

•February Columbia Swim Center closed for energy conservation.
•May 15 Senior citizen Evelyn Haynes and fellow gardeners win their battle to find a permanent site for communal garden plots. The ground is broken for the Elkhorn garden plots, just off Oakland Mills Road.
•June 18-July 5 A two-week celebration of the 10th birthday of Columbia, complete with a Pioneer's Dinner (for the first-year residents of Columbia), a Family Olympics and rededication ceremony.
•July The Columbia Pro Cantare chorus forms.
•Aug. 21 Centennial High School opens.
•Aug. 28 Hammond High School opens; its building duplicates Centennial's.
•Sept. 17 The first Renaissance Festival is held in Symphony Woods — replete with roasted turkey leg vendors, jugglers, and mud-wrestling.

1978

Central Library plans approved. Columbia Council takes on powers and duties of the Columbia Executive Committee, which is later abolished. Darryl Gee is the first Columbia athlete to go pro — he plays for the New York Cosmos soccer team. Tamini Paumier wins the silver in the Pan American games in Puerto Rico. Kings Contrivance joins the Columbia Council.

Debuts: Cable television; a solar research home built by Ryland in Kings Contrivance; Owen Brown Place, though the groundbreaking is snowed out.

•July 22 President Jimmy Carter attends a Willie Nelson concert at Merriweather Post Pavilion.
•Sept. 12 John and Claire Lea open J.K.'s Pub in the Wilde Lake Village Center. Along with the Leas, Longfellow natives help construct the watering hole. And the Wilde Lake High School football team helps hoist the dark wood hanging bar.
•Sept. 15 Slayton House is rededicated.
•Oct. 4 Owen Brown Village Center opens under Giant Food management, the only village center not managed by Rouse.

1979

James Rouse steps down as president of The Rouse Company; Michael Spear, who started with Rouse as a summer intern, assumes the helm. Mrs. Z's restaurant burns to the ground. Calendar Magazine starts publication. Columbia Horse Center moves from Route 108 to its new location on Gorman Road. The Rose Price House at Oakland Manor is renovated. The town votes not to pursue a municipal charter. Sears announces it is coming to the mall expansion. Toby Orenstein takes over Garland Dinner Theatre and renames it Toby's Dinner Theatre.

•Feb. 17 First residents move into Shalom Square, the interfaith housing endeavor for seniors, closely followed by residents moving into Owen Brown Place and Longwood.
•Feb. 19 A blizzard dumps 20 inches of snow on Columbia.
•March 9 Ground is broken for a new wing on Howard County General Hospital.
•March 26 The first radio show is broadcast from the New Town, on WLMD in the Mall.
•May 6 Groundbreaking for the Central Library on Little Patuxent Parkway.
•Nov. 1 Patuxent Publishing, which owns the Columbia Flier, buys the Stromberg string of newspapers — the Howard County Times, Catonsville Times, Arbutus Times, Booster and Reporter.
•Dec. 14 Dorsey's Search deed and agreement.

1980

Residents tie yellow ribbons around the People Tree in support of the hostages in Iran. Long Reach Library closes. The Columbia Association's "balanced budget by '85" cam-

1980: A model conceived in the early stages of Columbia's development depicts the urban environment that planners envisioned for the city in 1980.

paign begins. Dorsey's Search model home park is built.
Debuts: Columbia Hilton, the new town's second hotel; Chick Rhodehamel installed as Columbia Association's ecologist; Rusty Scupper restaurant

on Lake Kittamaqundi; The Supreme Court health club; MacGill's Common; Hobbit's Glen and Hopewell pools.

Statistics: 2,682 students at Howard Community College; 1,500 kids on swim teams; 2,000 kids playing on soccer teams.

1981

Columbia Association bows out of preschool and day care. Hobbit's Glen golf club is renovated. Dobbin Center and the Florence Bain Senior Center under construction.
Masses of apartment complexes convert to condominiums, but the County Council passes a guarantee of low-cost, three-year leases for disabled, elderly, and low-income residents.

Debuts: Huntington II model home park; Hawthorne neighborhood center; Cedar Lane School.

Statistics: 45 miles of pathway; 77 picnic areas; 101 tot lots; 1,312 acres of open space.

•January The Central Library opens with 1,263,966 books.
•June The graduations of the first kids to successfully complete 12 grades of school in Columbia.

1982

Columbia Council becomes the Columbia Association Board of Directors. Dorsey's Search joins the Columbia Council. Kings Contrivance model home park opens. The new owner of five Columbia apartment complexes is accused to trying to drive out low-income tenants; the county mandates new management policies. Columbia Bank and Trust merges with Equitable Trust.

•March Blue Cross/Blue Shield buys Columbia Medical Plan.

•March 4 Jamie Colleen Mace, a 2-year-old, drowns in Wilde Lake under a thin skin of ice near the dock.

•May 28 A twin-engine Beechcraft plane crashes into an empty house in Owen Brown. Four business travelers and the pilot are killed.

•Dec. 6 Vernon Gray, the county's former liquor board chairman, is sworn in as the county's first black council member.

1983

Merriweather Post Pavilion sustains $200,000 damage in a fire. Buyers camp out to purchase Howard Homes. The Environmental Protection Agency grants Columbia Association money to clean up the lakes. The Columbia Petting Zoo closes; all animals go to the Catoctin Mountain Petting Zoo.

1983: Columbia experiences its first Middle Age crisis as the Renaissance Festival gathers its wenches and knaves and heads for greener pastures in Crownsville.

Debuts: Dickinson model home park; pedestrian bridge over Route 29; Huntington and Dickinson pools; Florence Bain Senior Center; Dobbin Center; a parcourse fitness trail in Town Center; the student exchange with Cergy-Pontoise.

•May The Renaissance Festival decides to move

1983: Columbia's animal farm makes 1983 the last call for its goats. When the Symphony Woods attraction closed, the animals were moved to the Catoctin Mountain Petting Zoo.

to a larger site in Crownsville.

•Oct. 31 The Sewell family closes its 172-acre, pick-your-own farm. For decades, Howard County residents picked Sewell's Orchard's strawberries, apples, and pumpkins.

1984

The Columbia Council opposes councilmanic

redistricting for the county. Cergy-Pontoise dedicates Columbia Square in the French new town. Debuts: Towson State University holds first classes here; Columbia Archives; Dorsey's Search pool; Owen Brown Interfaith Center.

•Oct. 21-22 Nobel Laureate novelist Isaac Bashevis Singer in residence with Howard County Poetry and Literature Society. He reads on Sunday to an audience at Howard Community College. On Monday, he reads to and discusses with county high school students.

1985

Columbia Association's budget is balanced for the first time, as promised. The Grateful Dead visits Merriweather Post Pavilion for a 20th anniversary tour; Dead Heads bathe in fountains and streams and play Frisbee en masse in Symphony Woods. Columbia Council votes to develop Allview Golf Course land for townhouses and apartments. Flume proposed for Columbia Swim Center.

Debuts: Clary's Forest model home park; Columbia Magazine replaces Calendar.

1986

Columbia Association starts self-insurance program. CA purchases the Supreme Court. Construction begins on Winter Growth, the county's first adult day care facility.

Debuts: Splashdown flume and its insurance woes; the first Columbia Triathalon in and around Wilde Lake (Reg Hahn wins it); indoor tennis courts at the Columbia Athletic Club; Kings Contrivance Village Center; Parkview and Symphony Woods office buildings.

•Sept. 14 Pulitzer Prize-winning author and equestrian Henry Taylor delivers his poems from

atop a thoroughbred named Roman, after a spirited ride at the Columbia Horse Center.
•Nov. 4 Liz Bobo elected first woman county executive in Maryland.

1987

CA and The Rouse Company start a $6.3 million renovation of the Lakefront area in downtown; they sell bricks to residents imprinted with their names which are laid on the walkways. The Water Curtain opens to honor the relationship between Columbia and Cergy-Pontoise (located in front of the Parkview building on the Columbia Mall parking lot). The interchange at routes 29 and 108 opens.

•March Owen Brown Village Center expansion opens.
•May 23 The Hawthorne pool opens, complete with hot tub and cascading mushroom fountain.
•June 19 A parade and larger version of the City Fair celebrate the city's 20th anniversary.
•Oct. 31 The Rivers Park Fire Station is dedicated on Old Columbia Road.

1988

•January Patuxent Publishing Co., the publisher of the Columbia Flier, buys Columbia Magazine from Columbia Association.
•April 17 King's Contrivance Village Center opens.
•June International Peace Week, consisting of 200 Soviets and 200 Americans, stops overnight in Columbia.
•June 25 Dickinson pool opens.
•Aug. 7 The first Grand Prix horse-jumping event is held at Howard Community College. It nets $100,000 for the school's scholarship foundation.

1989

First woman is admitted to the Columbia Rotary.

•March 16 A huge retirement party is held for Ruth Keeton, who resigns as chair of the County Council after 23 years of service. She had developed Alzheimer's Disease.
•April The Rouse Company celebrates 50 years in business.
•May Frank Gehry wins the 1989 Pritzker Architecture prize; he is the architect for the Exhibit Center, Merriweather Post Pavilion, and the Rouse Company headquarters.
•June 23-25 First Columbia Festival of the Arts is held.
•Sept. 26 The first Howie Award is presented by the Howard County Arts Council to Norman and Nancy Winkler for their work on the Candlelight Concerts.
•Sept. 27 Dorsey's Search Village Center's grand opening.
•October Kmart opens in Dobbin Center, replacing Bradlee's. Columbia Memorial Park, the city's first cemetery, opens its gates.
•Oct. 14-15 The Prairie Ship Columbia is launched, marking a two-year study and celebration period by the Columbia Forum, dubbed the Columbia Voyage. Fourteen-foot-high sails are erected in a field near the Mall.
•Oct. 22 The renovated Oakland manor reopens, Columbia Association as landlord, for weddings, parties and meetings.
•Dec. 15 The Exhibit Center closes.

1990

•May The first annual Great Columbia Bike Ride is held. Princeton Sports and Piccolo's Ristorante are sponsors.
•May 12 Dickinson Park dedicated.
•May 26 Clary's Forest pool opens.
•Aug. 24 Michael Spear, the president of The Rouse Company, dies with his wife, Judy, and daughter, Jodi, when the plane he was flying crashes in fog near Boston. They are buried in Columbia Memorial Park.

1991

•June 15 The Columbia Forum holds the city's first Great Cardboard Boat Regatta, with 47 crews piloting corrugated cardboard boats around Lake Kittamaqundi. The Columbia Bank wins the Titanic Award for most spectacular sinking.

1992

•February A 6,500-square-foot addition is built onto Howard County General Hospital to accommodate the Magnetic Resonance Imaging Center, which performs advanced diagnostic testing.
•April Columbia Association launches 1st Place,

1993: Scientists place seismographs in Columbia after a series of earthquakes jolted the town's residents during the early spring of 1993. The quakes measured near 3.0 on the Richter scale, with no injuries or property damage recorded. (Photo by Jason Lee)

a new singles program which meets at the Oakland Mills Barn.

•October Patti and Roger Caplan are the first residents of the long-awaited River Hill village. Columbia Association opens the Welcome and Information Center in its new headquarters, the Teacher's Building on Lake Kittamaqundi.

1993
•March 10 A series of small earthquakes, averaging about three on the Richter scale, rock Columbia over the next few weeks.

1994
•June 19-20 Roland Flint and Garrison Keillor perform a two-hour program of poetry reading, from their own works, as well as verse from authors like Shakespeare, Housman, and James Wright. More than 750 people joined in song at the end.
•August The East Columbia Branch of the Howard County Library opens in Dasher Green.

Statistics: 29,831 homes (single family houses go for $155,000 to $800,000); 79,000 residents; average household income $72,150; 2,400 businesses; 55,400 people employed in Columbia.